Thomas Keith Tindale
South Hanover
July 1964

O MY AMERICA!

Notes on a Trip

by T. S. MATTHEWS

Simon and Schuster · New York

1962

LIBRARY OF CONGRESS CATALOG CARD NUMBER: 61-16559
MANUFACTURED IN THE UNITED STATES OF AMERICA
BY VAIL-BALLOU PRESS, INC., BINGHAMTON, N.Y.

To My Fellow Travelers, Omi and M.

O my America! my new-found land . . .
— JOHN DONNE

As an American, I naturally spend most of my time laughing.
— H. L. MENCKEN

Some people have chaos, and some have organization. Only the Americans have both.
— CLAUD COCKBURN

Indeed I tremble for my country when I reflect that God is just.
— THOMAS JEFFERSON

Naturally, in such a short trip, we had no opportunity to see how things were with the country or the people.
— ERNEST HEMINGWAY

My Country, 'tis of thee,
Sweet Land of Liberty,
Of thee I sing;
Land where my fathers died,
Land of the Pilgrims' pride,
From every mountain-side,
Let Freedom ring!

My native Country, thee,
Land of the noble free—
Thy name I love;
I love thy rocks and rills,
Thy woods and templed hills,
My heart with rapture thrills
Like that above.

Let music swell the breeze,
And ring from all the trees
Sweet Freedom's song;
Let mortal tongues awake,
Let all that breathe partake;
Let rocks their silence break—
The sound prolong.

Our fathers' God, to Thee,
Author of Liberty,
To Thee we sing;
Long may our land be bright
With Freedom's holy light;
Protect us by Thy might,
Great God, our King!

—SAMUEL FRANCIS SMITH

CONTENTS

1

De Tocqueville, Stand Aside

"One comes out every eight minutes," said M.

"One what comes out?"

"Another book on America."

"Well, it's quite a big subject still, so why not?"

"Well, *why?*"

...

"How do you think we should go about it?" said M.

"We could read some books."

"I've read some books."

"We could go there."

"I've been there. After all, we were born there."

"We could revisit. Middle West. Far West. South. That kind of thing."

"Well, why?"

* * *

"Let's take Omi with us."
"You know, I think *that's* a wonderful idea."

* * *

Omi was there already; she lives in St. Louis. She is a lady who describes herself as "quite grown up" —and she doesn't regard people as really grown up until they are seventy. While she was being a doctor's wife and the mother of four inquiring and obstreperous children, she was also trying to make St. Louis a better town. Not the best of all possible towns, since she is a woman and a realist, not a booster; but a community of civilized people, a place she can be proud of. The city's affairs have involved her with the state's as well, and her house-cleaning has spread all over Missouri. She has gone after ends that seem to her both practical and modest but that do not always look attainable to others (until Omi and her cohorts attain them): purer milk, wrapped bread, free clinics, better schools, smoke abatement, women's suffrage, the League of Women Voters, equal opportunities and rights for Negroes, improved marriage and divorce laws, better child labor legislation. All kinds of things. Inevitably, of course, she gets into politics. She has never held any public office herself, but her prestige in liberal-minded St. Louis is immense. Her civic firepower has been estimated as "the rough equivalent of six Marine battalions." In 1931 the Women's Advertising Club of St. Louis named her one of the ten outstanding women in the city; seven years later a St. Louis newspaper poll found her one of the five outstanding women in the whole country.

Unless you lived in St. Louis yourself, you could know Omi a long time without getting more than an inkling of all this. She isn't the embattled-club-woman or the crusading-social-worker type at all. True, she has a "Bryn Mawr voice"—clear but not strident, and quite un-Midwestern; she carries herself with natural and unconscious pride and is plainly unafraid of anything or any person. But she is not in the least aggressive. In fact, she is hopelessly attractive, to everybody. It isn't so much that she is pretty and sometimes beautiful (she is that) or that her blue eyes are often as appealing as a little girl's. The essential and peculiar thing about her is a quality which I can neither describe nor analyze, but it is something quite different from charm and good looks, and much more. When you're with Omi, you feel better about the human race.

Even her foibles are endearing. Never a day passes that she doesn't buy a present for somebody; she dashes off letters and postcards by the daily dozen to friends and family all over the world; and her telegrams (she's always sending birthday telegrams and cables) read just like her letters, for the simple reason that she never tries to save words. She doesn't always sign her letters, but that's not be-

cause she's forgetful but because she likes to vary
the ending; her letters often break off in a dangling
affectionate participle. She avoids wearing a hat
whenever possible. Instead she ties a narrow gray
ribbon around the coiled braid of her hair and
when she gets indoors takes off her hat by untying
the ribbon. Her combs are worn precariously and
often fall out; she weeps at movies, even bad ones.

She has no sense of direction, and she never fails
to lose her way in any strange town. When that
happens, a group of wishful helpers collects around
her; for there is something about her, like a fire on
a cold day, that attracts human beings of all kinds.
If she herself feels chilliness or tension in the air,
she talks—a kind of neutral babble that seems ir-
relevant but isn't. M. calls this "nattering," but it's
more like a rescue party. When it's a question of
her own convenience or comfort, the truth is not
in her.

She is certainly not a bit formidable, unless in a
deep sense—the sense in which faith, hope and
charity are formidable. Omi is not her real name,
but it suits her. M. is her daughter, and that suits
both of them. With Omi as our traveling companion, touchstone, compass and guide, how could
we go wrong?

In true Omi fashion, once she was persuaded to
come with us and to stay the course, she never
asked anxious questions about where we were going or why, or whether we were sure we were following a sensible plan. After she had told all her

committees and deputies to behave themselves and work hard while she was away (and privately determined to bombard them with letters to keep them up to scratch), she got ready to pack up and come along.

Her only stipulation, which we made for her, knowing that she wouldn't make it for herself, was that we should pay a visit to her beloved St. Louis before we set off on our journey. The date of our rendezvous there was mid-September.

...

First, M. and I joined forces in New York. Or rather, outside it; M. regards that city as the seventh circle of hell and had arranged to bypass it. She had been in Spain, looking as usual for a rentable castle; I had come on a few days ahead, as advance man.

At seven forty-five one bright fall morning I waited at Idlewild for M.'s plane (at last reported two and a half hours late; now they tell me!). A pretty name, Idlewild. But hardly appropriate to the place itself, which gives the impression of going somewhere, loudly and ostentatiously, without ever getting there. "Sky jump" would suit it better. In all the years I'd been coming here the only noticeable change seemed to be more and more half-completed buildings, a spreading of desolate concrete and bare wastes of earth. And why is everything so far apart? Transatlantic passengers like M. come in at the International Building and then, if they want a domestic airline, have to take a taxi to get there; it's much too far to carry their luggage—as any porter will tell them.

Is there a more inconvenient and uncomfortable airport in the world? (Yes, Chicago; I nearly forgot that one.) As for the "system," the Immigration and Customs bottleneck through which all incoming passengers have to squeeze, you can only say that it isn't quite so infuriating as the dingier version you encounter on the New York docks. At Idlewild, at least you don't have to line up for a Customs inspector and then, after he's finished with you, line up for a porter. On the other hand, the Idlewild system is to keep you and your luggage separated as long as possible: when at last the steel doors draw up and reveal to the ravening passengers the thoroughly helter-skelter dump of suitcases, the ensuing free-for-all is something to see.

From the glassed-in gallery overlooking the Customs floor I was seeing it now. As usual, the battle was going to the pushiest and strongest. M. was doing pretty well, for a lone woman, but her big suitcase, which she had finally unearthed, was too much for her, and I saw her looking frantically around for a porter. These elderly colored men were few, unavailable or unwilling; they plodded slowly past the edges of the ruckus, ignoring appeals for help. When M. gripped one by the sleeve I thought she had him, but he jerked loose, nodding curtly toward a stack of wire-and-metal carts, like the carriers you see in supermarkets. No doubt he was saying (the glass barrier made this tumultuous struggle a dumb show), "Help yourself, lady."

M. seized one of these carriers, a fellow passenger lent a hand in disentangling it from the stack, and she toppled her suitcases onto it. I wondered if she would notice that her cart bore a sign saying "Welcome" in seventeen languages. The last time I had been through this particular mill those signs had made a deep impression on me.

At last it was over, and M. and I met in the lobby and thankfully embraced.

"Welcome to New York."

"It's enough to kill an ox."

M. is not thoroughly adjusted to the electronic age. As we approached the outer doors and they swept open to let us out, she paused for an amazed moment instead of nipping smartly through, as I did, and the closing doors nearly got her. She seemed to regard this as a treacherous attack.

"Well, I never! What a thing."

I thought the rest of the day would be fairly simple, or at least downhill. Luckily, you never know. Our plane for St. Louis was due to leave Idlewild in a couple of hours. We took a taxi to the "domestic departures" building, a dingy and crowded shanty, one of those "temporary" structures still characteristic of airports, with an air of bedraggled flimsiness calculated to make dubious passengers like me feel that the air age is not yet here to stay. Still, we could get a cup of coffee and a sandwich and a drink in a jam-packed restaurant; and slowly the time passed.

At last we got aboard; our plane roared down the runway for the takeoff. Just when it should have been leaving the ground, it stopped with a slam of brakes. Silence. Then over the plane's loudspeaker the stewardess's plaintive Southern voice: "Please keep youah seat beyelts fayastened. Theah's been a sla-ight mechanical deficiency."

Presently we were back where we started. This time the restaurant was even more crowded, and much noisier. Four hours crawled by before our relief plane was announced.

It was well after dark, and we were numb with exhaustion when at last we shuffled aboard. We settled ourselves, we fastened our seat belts. Over the loudspeaker the stewardess apologized for our delay and thanked us for our patience and good nature. No sooner were we airborne than the captain, at greater length, apologized and thanked us.

The stewardess passed around a sheet of paper and asked us to sign our names and addresses. What for? So that the company could mail us another apology. M. and I said thank you, no, we'd had enough of that; we'd rather have a drink.

By this time, one way and another quite a lot had been drunk by the whole company, and the plane had become a picnic bus. Most of the passengers were like schoolboys dressed up as middle-aged businessmen; it was an uproar of shouts and grinning murmurs, slaps on the shoulder and visiting around. As background music we had baseball scores rasping from the loudspeaker.

"It's the end," said M. "Let's get drunk."

But we couldn't. Only two drinks, the stewardess said firmly, were served in flight, and we'd had them.

▀▀▀

It was wonderful to see Omi again. For several days we did nothing but warm ourselves in her presence. Then M., who is orderly, called a business meeting.

"What we have to do now," she said, "is plan."

That seemed a sound idea.

"From each according to its ability," said M. "I shall investigate the widespread happiness of Americans, the school system, juvenile delinquency and beatniks."

Then they looked at me. "I might put down some broad observations. Dotty but kindly. And superficial, of course."

"Let's hear one."

"Well, St. Louis is a city inhabited almost entirely by Germans, some of whom are French. There are also a good many Negroes."

"You'll have to do better than that."

Omi said, "I shall carry the booze bag."

2

The Whale and the Plankton

Our hotel was on Kingshighway, one of the principal avenues of the city but miles from downtown St. Louis—a good half hour by bus, or nearly two dollars in taxi fare. To get to the big department stores and office buildings in the old town that had grown up along the muddy banks of the Mississippi meant an expedition to be planned and timed. Our section of the city had its own shops and hotels but was mainly residential; unhurried, tree-lined streets with here and there a solid Victorian stone survival, some of them down-at-heel, some turned into apartments or stores, but a few still as well-groomed and massively plutocratic as ever. These few relics were inhabited by rich St. Louisans who had not followed the fashionable trend and moved into "the County"—out into the suburbs, to Clayton and beyond.

Like many other American cities and towns, St. Louis has stretched itself so far that its extremities have grown at the expense of its midsection, which is now largely abandoned to warehouses, seedy small shopkeeping and the poorer Negro population. This undistributed middle is gradually being reabsorbed into the city's growth, but the process will take years.

The front windows of our hotel looked across the street to the beginning of a great park, out of which opened a delta of roadways. In the lines of trees bordering the park there were gaps left by a tornado that had swept through some months ago. From a corner window we could see the hotel's big swimming pool. A newspaper had blown in and sunk to the bottom; through the clear water you could read the headlines on its drowned pages.

Omi had been worried about the weather we might encounter in September, and some of the time it was rather muggy; but M. likes heat and I like air conditioning, so we didn't mind. The weather, I noticed, was the one subject on which all the St. Louisans we met were defensive. Most of them declared that the damp heat of the summer and the raw wet cold of the winter were the only drawback to living in their town, and added that it was a price well worth paying.

▰▰▰

St. Louisans are very hospitable. There were a lot of parties.

M. said, "Goodness, I feel ill. It doesn't seem sane to start cocktail parties at five-thirty if you're not going to stop them and eat until nine-thirty. I wonder how they keep their health."

▄▄▄

"*Twenty*-ounce steaks," M. said. "Look, they write it on the menu by weight. Whatever next? It's hardly human."

▄▄▄

"No one ever speaks about money," M. said. "Have you noticed? I suppose it's common to mention it. But I want to talk about it every minute. I never saw such prices; how *can* people manage? Even only picking up a few bits and pieces in the drugstore is bankrupting."

"What did you buy in the drugstore?"

"Mexican jumping beans. Four of them in a dear little white plastic box with a glass lid so you can see them jump. I honestly cannot imagine why there would be any demand for Mexican jumping beans."

"Why did you get them?"

"For you. For company."

▄▄▄

"Facts are what you're weak on," said M.

"Facing facts?"

"No, *getting* them, remembering them, putting them down in your notebook."

"Yes, I guess you're right. The trouble is, the things I notice don't seem to be important. I saw a tiny car downtown today, with a printed sticker on its back window: 'Help stamp out Cadillacs.'"

"Exactly. Besides, that's old hat."

"Not to me it wasn't. And the menu of a restaurant where I had lunch was headed 'Gracious Dining since 1868,' and it listed 'Mumm's Cordon Rogue.'"

"You're hopeless, my poppet."

▲▲▲

"I'd forgotten about chewing gum," I said to M.

"How do you mean, forgotten?"

"How widespread it is. How indestructible. It never seems to lose its grip. And it's all over the place, you keep stepping on it. There must have been a wad of it in my locker at the tennis club. I had a hell of a time getting it off my sweater."

Another thing I'd forgotten about was conventions. There was one going on in our hotel when we arrived. The lobby and the elevators were jammed with delegates, each man sporting a large round card on his lapel, with his name, nickname and home town printed clearly on it. The whole hotel swarmed and hummed with ticketed delegates as they crowded purposefully up and down or in and out, greeting each other with great good will or clotting together in head-nodding, earnest converse. Signs posted by the elevators on every floor spoke of their daily program: morning get-togethers, luncheon meetings, afternoon outings, banquets. In three days this locust swarm had disappeared, and another immediately took its place. Now the badges on the lapels were yellow instead of white; the signs in the lobby no longer welcomed the Auto Salesmen but the Home Builders' Association. But the faces, the voices, seemed identical.

I started a list of Tempting but Uncheckable Generalizations: "Young American businessmen are overweight. Older American businessmen are more overweight (but they look more natural)."

━━━

Liberace was appearing at a night club in St. Louis, and Omi and M. and I went to see what we thought of him. Though I don't care for him myself, I'll be guided by the experience of a British friend of mine who, in the column he writes for a London newspaper, said exactly what he thought of Liberace, and it cost his paper £8,000.

Since Liberace is so well advertised, his face was no surprise, dimples and all, nor his velveteen tail coat and ruffled shirt, but his famous charm made rather a disagreeable impression on us. He seemed like a Little Lord Fauntleroy turned wise guy. The rest of the middle-aged audience gave him a good hand, but they didn't exactly go wild over him. One odd thing was the number of references he made to his victorious libel suit against that London paper. These remarks all fell flat; I'm sure almost nobody in the audience had ever heard of the suit or had any idea what he was talking about.

When the bill came we decided that the evening had been almost half worth it. M. and I agreed that Liberace was indeed a Great American Something. Omi said, "He plays the piano very nicely."

▀▀▀

A few days later I said to M., "You know, M., I like St. Louis."

"What do you like about it?"

"Well. Not the looks of it so much. It's a bit too disjointed, and pretty damn ugly in spots. But I like the trees and the quiet streets, and those enclosed blocks with the gateways and fancy names on them —gives you a feeling that these people valued private living. I like the *pace* of the city; it doesn't seem too frenzied, but they obviously get a lot done. And they seem responsible—not just proud of their town as it is, but willing to work to make it better. I think it's an *amiable* place. More amiable than—oh, Cleveland, or Philadelphia. Amiable and tolerant. Perhaps the mixture of French and Germans has something to do with it. Didn't a lot of the Germans come here in 1848? That was the year of the big wind in Europe. That must be where they got their liberal tradition—the *Post-Dispatch* and all that. Yes, perhaps it's the people."

"What people?"

"You mean I haven't been seeing the right people. I'd like to know why not. Look where I've been: the Missouri Athletic Club, the Media, the Noonday, the University, the St. Louis Country Club, the Racquet Club. I've been out to dinner in the County, I've played some tennis, and I've heard some fairly funny stories."

"Such as?"

"Here's one: Four men were playing golf, holing out on a green near a highway. A funeral drove by, and the man who was putting stopped, took off his cap and bowed his head; the others all followed his lead. When the funeral had passed one of them said, 'By God, Jim, that was a fine thing to do. I don't know many men who would stop in the middle of a game to pay their respects to the dead.' Jim said, 'Well, after all, we were married for thirty-two years.' "

"You think that's funny?"

"Yes, I do. Well, at the time, anyhow, it may have seemed funnier. Would you like to hear another?"

"No."

"Then let me tell you about the Racquet Club. They still don't allow any women on the premises, ever; and when a wife calls up to ask for her husband, the club servant always says he's not there and then goes and tells him. They have a special kind of bourbon called Wild Turkey, it's a hundred-and-one proof, and the smoothest thing you ever tasted."

"So now you think you know St. Louis?"

"I didn't say that; I just said I liked the people I'd met."

"You'd better meet some other people."

▬▬▬

That's something you can't help doing. As I constantly had to remind M., the baleen whale coasts along through the ocean with his big mouth open, and the plankton enter in nutritious shoals; he can't miss. In this way I swallowed (among others) three Negroes, four journalists, five businessmen, a taxi driver and a night-club proprietor. M. wouldn't give me good marks on any of them, as she said I was getting outside my bailiwick; but my feeling was that a whale has no bailiwick, just an open mouth.

▬▬▬

"Poor people are more honorable than rich people," said the Negro shoeshine man.

While I was wondering what there was to say to that, he began to tell me the story of Dives and Lazarus, with sly glances up at me to see how I was taking it. Perhaps he saw I wasn't taking it very well, which seemed to please him. He ended by quoting, with great satisfaction, "It is easier for a camel to go through the eye of a needle than for a rich man to enter the Kingdom of Heaven." (He got a little mixed up and said "harder" instead of "easier," but the effect was the same.)

I said, "What church do you belong to?"

"Baptists. The Vindictive Baptists. You a Catholic?"

"A sort of Catholic."

"Sort of Catholic. That sounds like Episcopalian to me."

I admitted it. He looked at me with scorn.

"Them celibates," he said. "That's no good. A man got to have women, and all men are alike that way."

＊＊＊

The Negro bus driver (up Lindell Boulevard to Kingshighway) stopped the bus, rose from his seat and bawled, "Everybody got to pay a dime who can't show a transfer. Show your transfers!"

We all meekly raised our hands, transfers clutched in fists. He glowered, took the tally and, finding no lawbreakers among us, drove wrathfully on.

＊＊＊

This kindly and civically self-conscious city has the second highest crime rate in the United States (the highest is Los Angeles). That means that there are more crimes committed—or reported—in St. Louis than in the nation as a whole. And the national rate is dizzying enough. These figures, published in the St. Louis *Globe-Democrat*, were attributed to J. Edgar Hoover, who as head of the

F.B.I. ought to know: Every four minutes in the United States there's a murder, a rape or an "aggravated assault"; every 1.9 minutes, a car stolen; every seven minutes, a robbery; every 46.4 seconds, a burglary.

I went to see a Negro lawyer, who made me uneasy by treating me as if I were as clever as he was, which I wasn't, and knew as much as he did, which I didn't. He blamed the prevalence of crime on the city government, the district attorney, the medical profession and public apathy. Many robberies, he said, were committed by boys and men earning more than a hundred dollars a week—not because they were poor but because they wanted a little more.

Religion? No help there. The churches aren't honest, he said. You might expect them, at least, to tell the truth about the size of their membership, but they don't. His colored Methodist church claimed a membership of four thousand and actually numbered a quarter of that. When he went to his pastor and suggested that the church ought to set a good example in this kind of thing, even if it meant admitting that their figures had been padded, the pastor said he wouldn't dare go to the bishop and own up to the true state of affairs, it would be as much as his job was worth; the church was giving the bishop a dollar a year for every member, and he'd rather continue to pay the $4,000 levy than admit the facts.

"Good times," said the lawyer, "have made everything worse."

* * *

The four journalists were very relaxed. We all had one drink before lunch, and talked small. I couldn't get them to talk any bigger.

"What's life-and-death?" I said.

"Not much of it around."

"Nothing really happening anywhere? No snarls in the welkin? No hairs in the soup?"

"That's about it, just the usual."

Then it turned out that there was something: the new "housing developments for lower-income groups" (in other words, the new slums) were turning out to be dangerous places to live. One of them had developed such a reputation that milkmen were refusing to call there in the early morning for fear of being robbed and knocked on the head. And the elevators in these buildings, stopped between floors, were a favorite place for rape.

But otherwise, all quiet along the Mississippi.

* * *

At my businessmen's lunch, two old-fashioneds apiece helped, but not enough to melt the ice. All six of us knew each other or had known each other, years ago; but now, as then, two or three did all the talking. The chief topic was the Princeton Triangle Club, an undergraduate dramatic society that puts on a homemade musical comedy every year and in the Christmas holidays takes the show on tour to half a dozen cities. St. Louis, the western-most point of the trip, is also the hospitable climax.

The Triangle show has an all-male cast, so a large part of the fun is watching the female im-personators, especially the beefy chorus, trying to look and dance like girls. At the final curtain, the whole company whip off their wigs, give a Prince-ton cheer and lead the audience in singing "Old Nassau." But it appeared that lately the boys had begun to take themselves a little too seriously, and at a recent performance in St. Louis they had re-fused to remove their wigs at the end of the show, on the ground that it would "spoil the illusion." This, added to some other uppity behavior, had resulted in St. Louis canceling the Triangle Club's visit the following year; now, I was told, the boys were back in line and the wigs came off in the good old way.

Just as we were getting up to go, the most talka-tive one took some printed cards out of his pocket and passed one to each of us. By the grin on his face I thought it must be a dirty story, and maybe the rest of them thought the same; anyway, we took the cards without reading them. Later I found mine in my pocket; this is what it said:

A DESKSIDE PRAYER

Slow me down, Lord! Ease the pounding of my heart by the quieting of my mind. Steady my hurried pace with the vision of the eternal reach of time. Give me, amidst the confusion of my day, the calmness of the everlasting hills. Break the tensions of my nerves and muscles with the soothing music of the singing streams that live in my memory.

Help me to know the magical, restoring power of sleep. Teach me the art of taking Minute Vacations . . . of slowing down to look at a flower, to chat with a friend, to pat a dog, to read a few lines from a good book.

Remind me each day of the fable of the hare and the tortoise that I may know that the race is not always to the swift; that there is more to life than increasing its speed.

Let me look upward into the branches of the towering oak and know that it grew great and strong because it grew slowly and well. Slow me down, Lord, and inspire me to send my roots deep into the soil of life's enduring values that I may grow toward the stars of my greater destiny. We always pray in the name of Jesus. Amen.

AUTHOR UNKNOWN

COMPLIMENTS

K. K. MADHAUSER, 1470 SHOSHONE BOULEVARD

I showed this to Omi and M.

"Don't you think it's beautiful?"

Omi, who doesn't hold with long-distance calls to heaven, smiled and said nothing.

M. said, "Minute Vacations. Pat a friend. Chat

with a dog. A few lines from a good book. Slow me down, Lord!"

Pretty soon we found we were all saying it.

▀▀▀

The taxi driver was white, and talkative. Boy, the things that went on in this town! He knew some districts where you could get anything you wanted—*anything*. Was he trying to impress me, or sell me something? When I said nothing, he tried again.

"Now, can you imagine this?" he said. "It's not indecent, but it's barbarious. A colored man was kissing a colored girl and he bit her tongue off. The police couldn't do a thing about it. Now I'm for equal rights, yes, sir, but that's going too far. Them colored folks ought to be kept in their place."

▀▀▀

"I don't think the Negroes here are very happy," I said to M.

"They're not privileged. Don't forget, we're looking for America at its best."

"I somehow get the feeling that under this kindly surface there's a certain amount of seething."

"You stick to the surface, my boy."

▀▀▀

The night-club proprietor was young and full of beans, and his wife was pretty. He talked "beat"— jive lingo which, not being a cat, I didn't always dig. The place they ran was an old-fashioned saloon, and they'd brought it up to date by making it even more old-fashioned, with chandeliers and carriage lamps and cluttered decorations from the horse-and-buggy era. Behind the narrow barroom was an equally narrow little theater where they put on a show, twice a night. The best act was two bouncy young Israeli singers, a boy and a girl, who sang well together and seemed to enjoy it.

The young pair who ran the place had written a satirical musical show, *The Nervous Set*, which had had a brief run on Broadway, and their ambition was to do another. Meantime he had done a scenario for a film, *The New Look Is the Anxious Look*. While I sat at the bar with his wife, M. talked to the proprietor. He told her a story she liked: a friend of his wanted to get married, but his father thought he was too young and advised him to live with the girl instead. Whereupon the son said, "Now, Dad, none of that old-fashioned immorality." He also told her what he would like from life. All he wanted, he said, was "economic security, women that smell good, and to do creative stuff."

▁▁▁

The four other guests had already arrived, and they were all having drinks on the terrace, in the hazy glare of the sun. It was a boiling hot day, and we'd have been much more comfortable indoors, but our hostess obviously wanted us to stay where we were. We sat and mopped our faces and drank bourbon on the rocks. After the second drink nobody minded much. The house was a modern architect's delight, all glass windows and horizontal planes and shouldering angles, with "functional" furniture and abstract pictures; everything matched. As we came indoors only our moving human figures flawed the perfection—looking as out of place, I thought, as manikins would if they came to life and strolled about a carefully designed show window, mucking up the composition.

At lunch the conversation was lively and soon grew warm. The question was, should the old post office be torn down or not? This building was one of the few in St. Louis that was more than a hundred years old, and it was architecturally "not bad": imitation classical but not fancied-up. Even our modern-architect host admitted that it had its points and had become a kind of monument to the city's past. It stood squarely in the midst of the downtown shopping district and was no longer used for anything.

"Why not a museum?" said M.

Land values were mentioned. Economic facts of modern life. City can't afford an idle building.

All lost on M. Or rather, waste motion. I look and listen expectantly while she clears for action. Now hear this. What about a sense of history? No awareness of the past? If you have a good thing, hang on to it. Crazy, wasteful destruction of everything "old," under the flimsy excuse of "progress, improvement." Real reason, money. Always money. Must "pay its way"! Why? *Why?*

Opposition alarmed, turns tail, breaks off action.

•••

M.'s favorite question is "Why?" She wanted to find a psychiatrist to ask him "one simple question": why are mental disturbances so widespread and growing in America—apparently more widespread and growing faster than anywhere else on earth?

The doctor was even more concerned than M. with this question, and his answer was alarming. As a people, he said, we have developed and encouraged the dangerous habit of trying to shut our eyes to the facts of death and suffering. In one of the city's largest and best hospitals, he said, many of the interns or resident doctors have never seen anyone die. And never will, if they can avoid it. We will do anything we possibly can to evade suffering, said the doctor. And we don't like passions: we substitute excitement for passion and sentimentality for love. Most of us can't bear to be alone, our lives are too empty. And since there's no general hardship to teach us, we run away from minor hardships or ignore them. So why shouldn't mental disturbances be widespread, and growing?

3

Omi's Town

M., student of privilege, looked at private schools, and didn't like much of what she saw. She seemed to be mainly sorry for the teachers, many of whom were bravely trying to rouse in their pupils a faint curiosity about life or learning; but she thought the children were overprivileged poops and phlegmatic doughheads. One teacher asked his class, "Are you all satisfied with everything you see about you? If not, what dissatisfies you?" No answer. And when they did speak she was sure their voices and slurvian accents should not be allowed.

"And why can't they speak in *sentences?*"

At several schools M. was asked to talk to some of the classes, and she did. After she had described an English school one boy said, "You might get a good education that way but would it make you into a well-rounded personality?"

⸻

"Guess what they were teaching fifteen-year-old boys in English class today? Eudora Welty. I ask you. Then there was a history class and as far as I could see they were romping through from the Egyptians to the Congress of Vienna in one year. How lucky Abraham Lincoln was to have nothing but a candle and the Bible, or was that what he had? Progress is really going to ruin this country; they better be careful."

Her purest scorn was reserved for the pupils at a fashionable girls' school. All they seemed to want was to get married—though a few said they might take a job in the meantime so they "won't just sit around"; and the experience would enable them to "help their husbands." One girl said she wouldn't mind marrying a man poorer than herself, if that fact didn't make him feel inferior.

M. was asked to address these girls, and must have pitched into them good and proper. Afterward one asked her if she was disappointed in Americans. Another took issue with M. and said it was hardly true to say that they didn't have hardships of their own, because they did—look at the term papers they had to write, and they rose to the challenge, "comparable to the Poles and the Hungarians." A third, who seemed to feel that M. wanted them to give something for nothing, said she didn't see why they should give up what they had, just because of all those underdogs in Europe.

The climax of M.'s inquiry into education came one evening when she met half a dozen professors, superintendents and teachers, the top people in the local universities and schools, who had been collected for her benefit. By the time I joined the party, the discussion of education had degenerated into a bickering argument, very like a quarrel, about how to be a good American. M. was being attacked from all sides, sometimes with venom, for suggesting that there was anything fundamentally wrong with American education. It turned out good Americans, didn't it? And what else was the point of being educated? How could an *American* learn anything from *Europe?* "French education turns out Frenchmen. English education turns out Englishmen. Thank God we're not anything like *them.* Aren't you proud of being an American?"

Walking home with M., I said, "What were they so angry about?"

"Me," said M.

...

"Americans don't seem to like *questions* about America," said M.

"Perhaps they feel that questions are the same as criticism."

"And criticism of America is un-American. Or anyhow anti."

"Well, isn't it?"

"No, damn it! It's our birthright. What do we pay taxes for?"

"Intercontinental missiles, mostly."

▰▰▰

M. went to call on a colored lady, very "upper-bracket." Her house stood on a tree-shaded street in a section of town that had once been considered a good address and was still genteel, though it had changed color. Her husband, whom she called "Doctor," owned two cars, a Cadillac and a Pontiac. The curtains in her living room opened and closed at the push of an electric button. Her kitchen was decorated in beige mother-of-pearl. She was stately, slow, grand and suspicious.

Her answer to M.'s "Why?" was prompt and downright. Advertising, she said, was to blame for everything that was wrong with the country. It appeared that children, captivated by ads, force their parents to buy a lot of stuff they don't want and don't need. "Children have to be satisfied." One of her neighbors, she told M., had been thus bullied into bankruptcy and was now in a mental hospital.

▰▰▰

"Everybody's happy," M. announced. "That's what they all tell me. They say they're just fine, it's just great, this is the pleasantest place in the world to live, everything's perfect. It fills me with suspicion. What about all the overworked psychia-

trists and the loony bins? Anyhow, happiness, that's
no way for grown-up people to talk. And the children in school: the important thing is to be adjusted to the group, and then you're happy. It
makes me very nervous. I'd hate to be adjusted and
I think it's an awful thing to do to children."

▄▄▄

No one could accuse TV in America of being a
serious subject—at least, I never heard anybody,
until the revelations about rigging quiz shows gave
the country moral hiccups for a whole week—so
I was allowed to take TV as one of my provinces.
I can't say I beat its bounds very thoroughly, but
that wasn't necessary. We had a TV set in every
hotel room on our trip, and in nearly all the motels. Even before we left St. Louis I was ready with
my report, a nice little list of broad observations:

  ➤ TV is boring, even to its moronic addicts.
  ➤ On most TV sets the reception is terrible;
  half the time, the screen shows a blinding
  snowstorm.
  ➤ The constant interruption of commercials
  is likely to induce nervous disorders.
  ➤ Nobody takes the commercials seriously.
  [*This* generalization, at least, was borne out
  by a scientific poll, which found that two out
  of three viewers took no stock in the ads
  whatever. As sales of the advertised products
  go up anyway, we can only suppose that TV
  commercials exert a subconscious effect which

viewers are powerless to withstand. So much for "sales resistance." Best not to brood on the implications?]

I remember only two occasions when the TV set made me sit up. One was when Khrushchev was on the screen, making his farewell speech at the end of his American tour. He'd been going strong for about ten minutes when the screen went blank and an announcer broke in to give the World Series scores. I kept tuned in for the rest of the speech, hoping it would happen again, but it didn't.

The other time was during a showing of one of the World Series games, when the sports commentator was telling us a thing or two about that day's pitcher for the White Sox. "Turk Lown got his nickname naturally, his first name being Omar."

"These Negroes, M."

"What about them?"

"I think they're pretty disagreeable, on the whole. Surly. Unmannerly. Disobliging."

"Remember how *they've* been treated."

"Yes. Yes. And still are. I don't suppose they can ever forget it. Just the same, do they always have to glare or look pot-faced? I don't think I like them."

"You're not supposed to *like* them. They don't like you either. You're just supposed to pretend they're the same as anybody else. Or that they're second-class citizens on their way up. Or that they're hardly there at all."

"You mean that's the American attitude?"

"Well, isn't it?"

```
▲▲▲
```

"He's in a temper," said M. "He had to fork out twenty-five cents for a fifteen-cent airmail stamp, and that put him in a rage."

"Omi, why is it so hard to post a letter in this town?"

"Is it? You can always get stamps at the post office."

"I can't find the post office."

"Each one has an American flag flying outside it. There's a branch post office only a few blocks from here, in a drugstore."

"First I tried to post them at the hotel," I said. "When I asked the girl behind the desk if she could mail these letters for me, all she said was, 'You can get stamps over at the newsstand.' I said, 'You can't mail them for me, then?' and she just repeated, 'You can get stamps over at the newsstand.' The woman at the newsstand had no airmail stamps, didn't know the postage rates to England and was nearly out of all kinds of stamps anyway. She told me to try the stamp machine in the hotel drugstore. I found the machine, and after careful study I put in two dimes, pulled the handle, and got two seven-cent airmail stamps and two two-cent stamps. These were wrapped in a bent piece of cardboard on which was printed (I copied it down): 'You never know when! Buy TUMS for the tummy for On the Spot RELIEF.' I then put a nickel in another slot and got four one-cent stamps, also gift-wrapped. I thus got my fifteen cents' worth of air-mail stamps, for which I'd paid twenty-five cents. I also got three one-cent stamps and two two-cent stamps which I didn't want."

"Don't shout," said Omi. "I'll show you where that post office is."

When Postmaster General Summerfield tried to cut down the Post Office deficit by curtailing a number of its services, the New York *Times* made an international survey of how postal services worked in other countries. It found that "three or four deliveries a day are routine in England, France, Italy and Japan" (against one a day in the United States); that "a Moscow citizen would find nothing extraordinary in twenty-eight mail deliveries to his door each week"; and that even in Spain, with two deliveries a day, the post office manages to make an annual profit of $4.5 million.

I saw one St. Louis, M. saw another. We got only a glimpse or two of Omi's. Once we went to a big meeting of the League of Women Voters, in the ballroom of a downtown hotel. Forty years ago, after she and her fellow suffragettes had won women the right to vote, Omi was one of the organizers of the National League of Women Voters, and now they and their numerous followers in St. Louis were celebrating the anniversary. The speeches were long, not a bit funny, and made you feel anxious and a little sad. Then at the end there was a surprise: Omi was given a present (a brooch) and had to make an unexpected speech herself. I had never heard her speak in public before, and I saw a new Omi. She was obviously saying just what came into her head, and what came into her head was just the right thing to say; she was forthright and funny without trying to be, and she never faltered. We all woke up and felt warm and alive again.

▄▄▄

And there was another glimpse when one evening she filled her small apartment with young nuclear scientists and their wives, some of whom were scientists, too. In the years she had lived there, Omi's apartment had taken on some of her character: it was cheerful and neat, bright, comfortable and welcoming. On the tables and bookshelves were framed photographs of people she loved, and orderly little piles of books she meant to read—and would, when she found time; classical engravings from the house she used to live in hung on the walls. Now the living room was pack-jammed with people, sitting on crowded-in chairs and sofas and all over the floor.

These experts were all concerned about the danger of nuclear weapons and the threat of fallout; the talk was fast and free, serious but far from solemn. Much of it was over the heads of the more elderly and nonscientific listeners, whose innocent queries were answered with varying degrees of patience. Omi was certainly the oldest person there, but they treated her like one of themselves. And it turned out that these young men and women were another of Omi's irons in the undying fire: a Committee on Nuclear Information, to inform the public of facts the government didn't always see fit to be frank about.

One young woman reported an odd problem. She was in charge of the collection of baby teeth from children born all over the United States since the beginning of nuclear tests; when large enough samples from the various regions were on hand the teeth would be analyzed for traces of strontium 90. She now had some sixty thousand teeth, all carefully filed and ticketed, stashed away in her attic. What would she do when she had no more room?

Then there was a discussion of what to do about factories making obsolete war material, things like fighter planes or old-fashioned high-explosive shells. If America should decide, as these young scientists hoped and believed it would, to shift this unnecessary arms production to peaceable plowshares, some competent mind would have to figure out—in order to save the manufacturers from bankruptcy and the workers from being thrown out of

their jobs—something else for them to turn to. The
one manufacturer present made no comment, but
his face was a study.

▪▪▪

It's not possible to measure the influence of one
person, but in St. Louis I kept encountering such
frequent traces of Omi that I began to give her unlimited credit for everything I liked about the city
—even such farfetched phenomena as the cheerful
manner of the waitress in our hotel dining room
("Sherr!") or the beauties of the Art Museum
(where one of the guards, delighted to hear M. ob-
jecting to some modern pictures, told her, "I
thought I saw a kindred soul. My private word for
it is the splash-and-splatter system").

▪▪▪

Having lived, or at any rate moved and had my
being, in New York for thirty years, I have thought
a good deal about what makes a city pleasant or
unpleasant to live in. The attractions of New York
are few but forceful and would be obvious even if
they weren't well advertised. The city's greatest
attraction is the excitement it engenders.

From the air New York looks like a crowded
graveyard, but at street level you feel the pressure,
the concentrated energy of the skyscrapers; the
taut streets hum with their power. New York's
beauty—and parts of it are beautiful—is of the
same galvanic kind: long, sharp-edged vistas that

make you catch your breath as if you had touched a live wire. These sudden glimpses, all man-made, give the impression of having been contrived recklessly, by accident. But no visitor and no inhabitant can escape the sense of being in one of the world's capital cities.

Then look at the faces of the people—tired, worried, suspicious. Listen to their voices (harsh) and the words they use (ugly). Ride a Bronx express at the rush hour. Read the *Daily News*, the city's favorite newspaper ("Look out, bud, they're gonna gyp ya"). Stand in Times Square; walk through the midtown fur district, or Harlem, or on the streets along the docks. It's a tough town, mister, sure is, in all kinds of ways, from Fifty-second Street up and down. New Yorkers like it that way, or say they do. Would *you* want to live there? You can see by the daily obit page in the *Times* that it's a place where a lot of successful men get their deaths, in their fifties or earlier. But how about living? Few people I knew would have chosen New York as a place to live; they were there because of the job. That incurable city, that crammed-up building site in a constant, unappeasable state of erection, that perfect though unfinished shrine to the bitch goddess—only *The New Yorker* can pretend that Manhattan is just a nice town at heart, a little smarter, a little quicker on the uptake than other towns. No, New York is unique, thank God. And as the song says about "that old graveyard," it is a nasty place.

Thanks to my long exile in New York it was gradually dinned into me that the city I should like to live in would be in almost every particular New York's opposite. It would not be noisy. It would not be on a continual rampage of tearing itself down to build itself bigger. It would have a fairly low and regular skyline, great squares, a sense of peace and enough room, trees lining its streets, and many parks. The anxious, urgent, driven pace would be lacking. Traffic would be more sedate, and pedestrians in less of a hurry. The whole atmosphere of the city, the tone of its life, would be gentler. There would be enough taxis, of the old-fashioned sort where the driver is shut off from his passengers, and you would not be compelled to listen to a homely philosopher just because you were paying for the privilege of riding in his cab. The public transport, the buses and subways, would be cleaner and the passengers would be treated like human beings, not cattle. In such a city it would be more comfortable, more convenient and much pleasanter to live.

London seems to me the city that comes nearest to filling that bill. But you don't have to travel as far as that to find significant demurrers from New York's way of life. One of the best things about St. Louis, I decided, is the ways in which it differs from New York. More space, more parks, more trees. In New York, civic pride runs a poor second to the jostling of giant corporations. Robert Moses has said that the spiraling chaos of congestion in midtown Manhattan is hopelessly out of control because the city is powerless to keep private enterprise within the bounds of sanity. Every time a new skyscraper is built or a bigger one replaces a smaller, more thousands of people are drawn into the already overcrowded area; public transport, already near the breaking point, must expand further, and the nearly intolerable congestion becomes more nearly intolerable.

St. Louis still has the civic pride that New York —its land values being what they are—can no longer afford. The privileged citizens of St. Louis, who certainly enjoy their privileged position, feel a corresponding responsibility to work for their town. They may not all be as tirelessly concerned with the *res publica* as Omi is, but they are concerned.

▲▲▲

In this most barbarous of all ages (will it really have to be called "the American Century"?), when life for the vast majority of earth's inhabitants has been more miserable and more brutish than ever before, when the cause of death in millions of recorded cases—and in millions more of unrecorded —has been man's inhumanity to man, we crave the reassurance of simple goodness. Americans are perhaps too simple for their own good; but they are good. Who can travel through America—especially if he heads West—without encountering again and again the unmistakable evidence of decency, kindness and generosity?

There are bastards in all countries (as a Virginian friend of mine says, "vultures in human form and sons-of-bitches unworthy of the name") and America is a big country and has its share of them; but I believe there are as many good people here as anywhere on earth. Since they are also my people, I think I like them better and feel more anxious about them and resent the bastards among them more than any foreigner could.

▀▀▀

"If you don't live inside America," M. said, "Americans regard you as a foreigner anyhow. Or worse."

"That's a postwar attitude, and very suspect and slimy, and has a lot to do with saluting the flag and taking loyalty oaths and making loud advertising patriotic talk about being American."

"Myself," said M., very lordly, "I dislike all governments. And I don't like whole nations at a gulp. I like bits and pieces of every one, some more, some less. There are moments when you sound like a nationalistic type."

"I'm an American type. It's not a thing I could ever lose and I wouldn't want to lose it."

▀▀▀

"Seriously, M., I do like this town."

"It has its points, I agree. But would you like to live here?"

"I can think of a lot worse fates. It might be very pleasant. The people. The university. The Art Museum. The *Post-Dispatch*. Omi. I'd rather live here than New York. Much."

"I should hope so. But *live* here?"

"Yes. Why not? Anyway, I'd like to want to."

"Sometimes I feel like Balaam," I said.

"Which one was Balaam?"

"My God, M., don't you know *anything?* Balaam was a kind of minor prophet in the Old Testament, and when the Children of Israel were on the rampage, one of the Canaanite kings they were pushing out of the way, I think his name was Balak, tried to use Balaam as a desperate last resort. He got Balaam up on a mountain, where he could see the Children of Israel coming. Balaam was supposed to curse them, which Balak hoped would either wither them up or turn them aside. Then there was a complicated bit of business with an angel and Balaam's ass, which I won't bother you with, but the upshot was that Balaam lifted up his voice and started to put a blessing on the Children of Israel, instead of a curse. At this point the horrified king tried to stop him and said, 'Neither bless them at all nor curse them at all'; but by now Balaam had the bit between his teeth and went ahead and blessed them from hell to breakfast."

"And that's what you're going to do, you minor prophet? Put a blessing on this tribe?"

"Yes, I would if I could."

⁂

"Would you like to sum up?" said M.

"What, already?"

"You ought to be able to wrap up St. Louis by now."

"I almost wish it were my town."

"It's Omi's town."

4

Newness of Life

We are a notoriously discontented people—notwithstanding the big bluff, the hearty lie, of our shifty-eyed optimism. Take the small matter of our national anthem. Other nations make do with theirs, no matter how drearily hymnlike they may be. We Americans have never felt easy with "The Star-Spangled Banner."

For one thing, nobody can sing it but a virtuoso; for another, very few of us can do more than hum it beyond the first verse; as the once popular (and now hushed-up) song has it, "None of us know the words but the Argentines, and the Portuguese, and the Greeks." On solemn occasions we hire a soprano to sing it, while we stand and listen, with our hats off: its rendition has become a spectator sport.

I suppose the reason why "The Star-Spangled Banner" was made official was because "America" ("My country, 'tis of thee") copied the tune of "God Save the King." And we find it convenient to forget that our chosen anthem borrowed its music from an eighteenth-century British drinking song and so is equally alien.

Most of us, I think, if the choice were left to us, would rather sing "America." I would, anyhow. Its words affect me more patriotically than those of "The Star-Spangled Banner," which have always struck me as chauvinistic and at the same time almost defeatist. What kind of satisfaction can you take out of being shelled all night by a British fleet and then simply seeing that your flag was still there in the morning? As every American knows, that's no way to run a railroad, or win a battle either. Let the British say, "It's dogged as does it." That's not the way we feel. It's un-American.

And the War of 1812, with which "The Star-Spangled Banner" is inevitably linked, still rankles in our memory—not only because we feel that it was not a clear-cut success for American arms, but because the bloody British hardly remember it, or remember it only as a small sideshow in the long struggle with Napoleon.

"America," on the other hand, rises above wars and rumors of wars and sings in grander if more platitudinous terms about our common country. There are some lines in it that used to make my scalp prickle:

I love thy rocks and rills,
Thy woods and templed hills . . .

What did they mean, those words? I knew what
rocks and rills and woods were, but "templed
hills"? I had never seen such a thing, except in imagination. It seems to me now that what the writer
must have had in mind were the white-painted
wooden churches of New England. The ones I remembered were not on hills but on flat village com-
mons; still, I took that as poetic license, and I got
the picture. It is a regional picture, however; I can
see that it might seem strange and even foreign to
Americans who live west of the Mississippi.

Perhaps America has outgrown its anthems, official and unofficial. A land that includes Texas and
Oregon, Arizona and California, needs a bigger
song, something on the scale of Walt Whitman. Or
must it be Irving Berlin? Anyhow, *singable*.

▚▚▚

I am sitting in a roomette on a train going west
from St. Louis to Denver (a bit over a thousand
miles). I've just had an enormous dinner in the dining car, and I have set my watch back two hours
—that's what you get when you go west in this
world.

For a couple of hours the train has been careen-
ing along the banks of the wide—well, fairly wide
—and powerfully rushing and muddy Missouri.
No Indians. I've been wondering whether the New

World isn't perhaps a very very old land that has swallowed up previous invaders with scarcely a trace; and whether the uneasiness of Americans may not come from an unformed suspicion that others have been here before us and left no echo.

At any rate, we've certainly got the surface licked. The train rattles on at about sixty m.p.h. My roomette measures six feet two by four feet, and in that compact space I have an upholstered seat with arm rests—big enough for me and a very small Lolita, if she half sat on my lap; a sliding door on my right, a large window with Venetian blinds on my left (also built-in ashtray and reading light); air-conditioning controls ready to my right hand; convenient to my feet an upholstered footstool— raise the lid and there's the W.C.; next to it the compactest washbasin you ever saw (h. and c., towels and soap hidden in smartly concealed crannies, and a special tap for ice water). Opposite me a large mirror, for making faces in, and over it a luggage rack and a special locker in which to leave my shoes, for overnight polishing. When I want to go to bed I stick my tail out into the corridor and heave on a certain handle, whereupon a made-up bed magically rises from the place where I've been sitting.

I love trains, particularly American trains—the good ones. This one is only so-so, but I'm grateful for it: for its slowness and comfort, compared to plane travel; and because, they tell me, it will soon be a thing of the past. The railways generally lose

money on their passengers and are said to hate
them. That's often mutual, as I know from twenty
years' experience of the Pennsylvania ("God damn
the Pennsylvania Railroad"). They have cut down
their passenger service as much as they dare; the
famous Twentieth Century Limited has been taken
off. In ten years—could it be true?—no more passenger trains in America.

▰▰▰

"Newness of life"—that magical phrase that
shines out, like a shaft of promissory sunlight, from
the encircling gloom of the Prayer Book's General
Confession. You can see what the words mean, and
that their magic exists and prevails, when your ship
runs out of the gray North Atlantic in January into
the fresh blue seas of the southern latitudes. And
you feel that same newness when you first breathe
the crystalline, mile-high air of Denver or see the
milky blue of a winter morning in southern California. This miracle of light has more in it than
meets the eye; it invades the mind like a rush of discovery, it lifts the heart. Obviously the sensation
wears off, so perhaps it's not a miracle after all. The
inhabitants seem to be used to it. Their boasts about
this climate they have been lucky enough or clever
enough to find are often indistinguishable from
Chamber-of-Commerce rant about the booming ex-
pansion of their ugly and embryonic cities.

And yet I wonder. Why did they come here in
the first place? And why do they stay? No matter

how the inhabitants put it—and they don't express themselves very well—I think their bragging or their awkward excuses don't do justice to their real reason for living here: the glorious light, the space and clarity of the Western air, which salutes them every day with "newness of life."

▴▴▴

Denver, they say, is where the West begins. Looking down from a plane, you can almost persuade yourself that you see the land beginning to tilt up toward the Rockies. From the window of my train the countryside looked flat, but overnight winter had come; although the sun was blazing in an enormous sky, the ground was creamy-thick with snow. I spent a couple of hours in the train's observation dome, which I had all to myself, watching for a first sight of the mountains. Near Colorado Springs I saw them, declaring their tremendous silent announcement, snow-topped outposts of the great ranges behind. And as we snaked around a curve in the single track, a glimpse, half hidden by the folded hills, of a regiment of long horizontal gray buildings, with the Stars and Stripes flapping from a tall flagpole: the West Point of the Air Force—the nursery of the future American samurai?

In Denver it was forty degrees colder than it had been in St. Louis. My old friend S. met me at the station. A very old friend. Our matter-of-fact greeting masked the shyness of two men who had known each other well as boys but who were now nervously aware that both of us must have deviated out of all knowledge. I think we were each relieved to find that we had not forgotten each other completely. As for what we had become, of course we were mutually disappointed. He thought I had failed to follow my natural bent: he had wanted me to be a modern J. Fenimore Cooper, a tall teller of tales. And I thought his luck was bad: he had been a judge, for which he was obviously well suited, had retired into the practice of law to make more money, and now, at the point in life when he should be settled in his career, wanted to return to the bench but couldn't get elected.

Why on earth *elect* judges? You might as well elect doctors, or dentists, or officers in the Army and Navy. And in fact, I remembered, that's how it was in the militia, not so very long ago: that was how Lincoln got his captaincy in the Black Hawk "war."

Anyhow, when we go as far as electing judges, we've let democracy run away with us. I suppose we began it in a revulsion from the way things were done in eighteenth-century Europe, all by royal edict or the patronage of the great. It may have been a laudable experiment, like Prohibition, but it too was based on a false idea: that the best man for *any* job can be chosen by popular vote. It seems an obvious enough principle, that the judiciary and the electorate should be as strictly separated as church and state. We had started McCarthy on his way to the Senate by electing him a judge. Was he ever a fit person to sit in judgment over other Americans? The horrible and still undigested fact is that later, when he set himself up as judge over all his fellow Americans, half the country said he was fit, or were afraid to say he wasn't.

I thought of Joe McCarthy on the bench to which we had elected him, and then of the bench to which my kindly, wise and experienced friend S. could not be elected—although he was certainly fitted for it and might well have been appointed to it. We know enough to appoint judges to all our higher courts. Then why do we make the great majority of our judgeships political offices, as if justice were mostly a minor concern of party politics? I can think of only two answers, one worse than the other: because the election of judges has become a sacred American tradition, no matter how senseless; or because at bottom we do not really respect law.

•••

During the three days I was in Denver I carried out my usual conscientious investigations: I played tennis, had dinner at the country club, where S. and his wife took me, and spent the evening hours drinking with them and their friends. Between times I moseyed around the city.

The layout of Denver is even more sprawling and disconnected than St. Louis'. If cities are in fact organisms, subject to the laws of organic growth, to what sort of living thing can we compare them? A sociologist has likened Chicago to a clumping of cancer cells. Then what is New York but a hardened artery? And Los Angeles a malignant tumor running wild? As for smaller and more easily observable organisms such as Denver, St. Louis, Phoenix or Dallas, they seem to resemble an embryo in its jellylike early stages, with here a blob and there a bit of cartilage, the whole messy conglomeration bearing only the sketchiest of likenesses to what the matured organism may become.

Denver, like the others, has its cozy, settled areas: tree-lined avenues, quiet enclaves of bungalows and solider stone houses, with scraps of lawn and little flower beds. These streets have no particular character of their own, they are not distinguishable from the "residential sections" in any other American town except by small variations in the style of the houses and by the type of trees (when there are any); but they give off a sense of village neighborliness, of homely order. They are peaceful, settled islands in the sprawl and heave of the disordered city. Between them and "downtown" lie gulfs of empty lots, reefs of jagged, jerry-built streets, the occasional outcropping of a new hotel or bank or apartment block. In the downtown area the new buildings are more numerous, but the early settlers of brick and brownstone still far outnumber the newcomers.

Another old friend had his office in the Zeckendorf Building, 1700 Broadway, one of the largest, shiniest and newest in Denver. I walked through glass doors into a sparkling lobby, floored with polished stone, and beyond it into a sunken plaza with a splashing fountain and colonnades of square silvery-metal pillars. In the wall at one end a bronze plaque was fixed. Its inscription read:

> *O God, our help in ages past,*
> *Our hope in years to come.*

My friend B., a native of Denver and a seasoned newspaperman, was as brisk and sardonically cheerful as ever. He was obviously at home with his job and his city. I asked him what he thought of the reporting of Khrushchev's recent visit to America. It seemed to me that the press had badly underestimated the impression Khrushchev had made. Was it in fact an honest underestimation? It looked to me more like a tacit agreement to discount a disquieting possibility. The newspaper reports I had read, like the commentators on radio and television, were unanimous in declaring that nobody in the United States had been taken in for an instant by Khrushchev and that he had shown himself as the wholly sinister figure he was. The unanimity of this press line, and the undertone of anxiety in its constant reassurances, made me wonder.

Wasn't there something about this coarse, shrewd, ruthless and energetic little bandersnatch that Americans recognized not only as familiar but also as attractive? It might be blasphemy to liken

him to Harry Truman; it would not be blasphemy
to compare him with Spyros Skouras. In fact, it was
impossible not to, for these two successful upstarts
had had a public encounter, emblazoned on the
front pages and recorded by the press cameras. At
a banquet in California, tendered to Khrushchev by
the tycoons of Hollywood, while the guest of dubious honor was treating the audience to his usual
mixture of long-windedness and heavy boasting,
Skouras interrupted him, snatched the microphone
away and got in a few heavy brags on his own account. For a moment there was almost a scuffle between these bald, fat, aging little men. Then Khrushchev regained possession of the microphone, took
a firmer grip and boasted triumphantly on. As an
exhibition of manners it was deplorable on both
sides, but the inescapable point was that Skouras
was less effective; he came off second-best. Americans don't like losers.

Then there was another scene, this time on a
Midwestern farm, where Khrushchev's host lost
his temper with the crowding press photographers,
shouted at them and tried to drive them back by
throwing clods. Khrushchev, roaring with laughter,
cheered him on. This incident too had its uncomfortable implications. How much better if it had
been Khrushchev, the tyrant and antidemocrat,
who had been infuriated at the liberties taken by a
free press.

We all felt very much relieved when Khrushchev's visit was over and he was safely gone,

without anyone having taken a pot shot at him or even heaved a ripe tomato. Nevertheless, it was an anxious time, and not just because we didn't want him snickersneed on the premises.

Why had he been allowed to come at all? A year before, six months before, it would have been un-thinkable—just as it would have been unthinkable a few months later, when Khrushchev's devilish-ness wrecked the summit meeting in Paris. It would have been hard to imagine Khrushchev's visit with Dulles still alive. And that's how it had happened: he had come over Dulles' dead body. With Dulles we all knew where we were, within the strict limits of our Presbyterian policy, and we knew, from the President down, that we must not even give the ap-pearance of fraternizing with the powers of hell. And now look: here comes Old Nick in person, as the official guest of the United States. No wonder there's some confusion in our American minds. From being hard-shell Presbyterians we have sud-denly become soft-shell agnostics. We hardly know what to think. Old Nick Khrushchev doesn't make it any easier for us. The worst thing about it, and we don't say it even to ourselves above a whisper, is that we recognize in him some traits that are characteristically *American*.

Have we really supped with the Devil? And if so, did we have a long enough spoon? Or worse still, have we seen the future, and does it talk Rus-sian but look like us?

Very little of this, or perhaps none of it, I said

to B., but at any rate he seemed to agree with me that Khrushchev had made an impression on plain people in America, and that the press had combined to ignore, deny or falsify the alarming fact.

▴▴▴

My Denver taxi driver was elderly; uncommunicative, but in a kindly way. We rode for miles through lanky streets in silence. Then he switched on his two-way radio. The usual metallic yammer from a voice at headquarters, calling cars by number, naming the next rendezvous; monosyllabic replies from the drivers. Gradually the monotonous drone took on a petulant note, the answering voice grew voluble and angry. At this point my elderly driver unhooked his microphone from the dashboard, raised it to his mouth and said, *"Shhhhh!"* The altercation ceased.

A few minutes later we were in a busy downtown street. The car ahead of us braked so suddenly for a red light that my driver had to jump on his own brakes. He stuck his head out the window and cursed the country driver with freedom and conviction; then turned to me and said, "Pardon my—exuberance."

▴▴▴

After three days Omi and M. rejoined me. M. asked me about Denver.

"It's on tiptoe," I said. "One foot, anyway."

"Be more specific."

I consulted my notes. "Here. I saw this sign in a restaurant window: 'Try our soon-to-be-nationally-famous Broiled Chicken Beurre Noir.'"

M. looked at me kindly. "On to Seattle," she said.

5

I Love Thy Rocks and Rills

The plane trip to Seattle took four and a half hours, and brought out the awed observer in all of us. M. scribbled notes:

"Olive-drab land—where scarred, rusty red. Snake of r.r. track. Then rock, like scabs, knobs of exposed bone, or old knuckles. Cloud shadows. Suddenly a town on the flatness (why there? or anywhere?). Right angles of streets, and a hint of this new thing, colored roofs. No center to a town, unlike Europe or Mexico; no meeting place. Land looks like a relief map, unlived-in and unlivable.

"Perhaps one would understand Americans if one understood the land, all of it; and every smallest detail of the history."

After a while we got tired of looking. M. and Omi talked.

"I want to talk about the American woman," said M.

Omi looked alert. Omi has spent her life working with American women and has a high opinion of them.

"If you read about the American woman," said M., "in foreign papers, magazines or books, you get a very clear picture, a unanimous picture, you might say. The American woman is, above all, powerful; she has the money, she controls the destinies of the men and the morals of the nation, she is a diamond-studded bully who may also be very beautiful. Does the group agree with that summary?"

We waited.

"I take it you do not read foreign opinions," M. said with dignity. "Now here I am and though of course I may not be seeing The American Woman I have seen a lot of American women. It is my impression that the girls are little better than Arab females and I would not be surprised to see them putting their hands under the gents' feet and saying 'Order, master, and I will obey.' Doing the same to the children."

Omi sighed, lightly.

"They spend their time driving their children to and from school; this is the basic chauffeur aspect of the American woman. They spend the rest of the morning doing their housework and marketing; this is the cook-and-charlady angle. They call for their children again but, if there is a moment to spare between the vacuum cleaner and the car pool, they go to meetings and the meetings are all admirable, looking after the life of the community or the world. When the kiddies have been washed, fed and tucked in, and a baby sitter has been obtained, they might be able to go to a lecture, preferably educational, in order to make themselves better informed for the benefit of their children or the community. If they are out on social occasions, it seems to me they defer very sweetly to their husbands; I'd go so far as to say they are building up the men's confidence. By the way, why does everyone need so much confidence in this country? The picture of the beautifully preserved bully escapes me. If I had to work as hard as most of the women I see, and notably the young women, I'd go into a decline."

"Yes," said Omi, in a neutral voice.

"The only really bad, stupid thing I can see that the American woman does is to shop. It looks like a mania, like being addicted to roulette, or opium. Perhaps they visit stores the way other people visit museums. But they do buy, I watch them buying absolute damned nonsense, which is neither beautiful nor useful. You will be fascinated to hear that you can, for instance, buy a bottle opener with a mink-covered handle. However. Now, I wonder about this. Do they shop because they are bored and it is an escape? Do they shop because of status seeking, which everyone says is a national occupation?—'I bet you haven't got a mink-handled bottle opener.' Do they shop because they are enslaved by advertising, which also everyone says is a national disease? Do they shop because their children are enslaved? I haven't an idea; I only note that they certainly shop and shop and shop, and it isn't normal. In the higher brackets and the older age group, it seems to me many women drink too much; I mean, it shows. But then, their men drink too much, so maybe they are keeping up; if everyone is going to slur their words, it's less tedious and less embarrassing to be in the same condition. But on the whole, I don't know what foreigners are talking about; The American Woman they describe must be a half of one per cent of the population."

"Oh, my child," said Omi.

"What do you mean, Oh, my child?" M. asked.

"I was thinking about generalizations," Omi said. "And how difficult they are."

"All generalizations are idiotic," said M. "But everyone on earth ends by talking and thinking them. That's to say if they talk or think. All right, we'll leave The American Woman."

Long before we got to Portland, the first stop, we would have liked something to eat, but the stewardess couldn't even give us a sandwich. Nor any drop to drink—except a cup of watery coffee.

```
```

Our hotel in Seattle was crowded and noisy with a convention, this time female: the Convention of the Supreme Emblem. That's what the cardboard

sign outside the ballroom said. The women themselves all wore engine drivers' caps and big round
buttons bearing the name of their home towns. And
they were mostly big women, big-bottomed, big-
breasted, with cheerful, strident voices that seemed
a little larger than life. We squeezed into an eleva-
tor with half a dozen of them; their badges read
"MIAMI." A mild-looking man wedged among
them asked mildly, "Miami, Florida?" In indignant
unison they shouted, "No—*Arizona!*" And they
were still babbling praises of their native town
when we wriggled out and left them.

We went to the bar for a drink before dinner.
The waitresses were Chinese, trim, dainty and
pretty as porcelain, and wore Chinese costume.
They looked much finer clay than the bedizened
women they were waiting on. M. said in her pierc-
ing whisper that *they* were the kind you'd expect
to see in barrooms in the Yukon.

It was raining next morning when I went to get
our first rented car. The simplicity of this opera-
tion was almost alarming. I showed my driver's license, signed a paper and was introduced to my car,
which seemed to me enormous and brand new: a
1959 Ford, green and white, with black-and-silver
cloth upholstery. The garage man waved me off
casually, but I wouldn't go until he had explained
all the unfamiliar gadgets on the dashboard and
beneath it and had given me careful directions for

finding my way back to the hotel through the steep one-way streets. Then I crept cautiously out into the rain-swept traffic.

It was only a Ford, I kept telling myself, and I had driven Fords for years. Yes, but they weren't half the size of this monster, with its automatic gearshift and its rows of unfamiliar knobs and buttons. Was that damn brake really off? When I drove slowly under the portico of the hotel, Omi and M. were waiting for me, and were gratifyingly impressed. One feature of our car that pleased us all was its trunk: it was spacious enough to swallow all our baggage.

We had made up our minds to travel light, but then, thinking of the different kinds of weather we'd have to dress for, and the necessity of books, and my tennis things, we persuaded ourselves that it would be all right to be overweight on planes, since we could carry any amount when we got a car. By this time we had collected between us eight bags, not counting lesser parcels: each of us had a big suitcase and a small one for overnight; there was one for our books (this weighed a lot), and the booze bag.

The big ones were a problem. They were rectangular and unyielding, they were made of some material that looked and felt like heavy cardboard or plywood but was actually as tough as elephant hide; it had been designed during the war for containers that were dropped by parachute. M. had bought the suitcases some years ago at a small shop in New York which was supposedly the only place in the world where you could get them. They were hideous and unwieldy, and, though very light when empty, they weighed a ton when full, since they held as much as a small trunk.

By the time we got on the Bremerton ferry the rain had stopped. We were headed for the Olympic Peninsula, where the American Automobile Association had warned me the weather would probably be bad at this time of year (October) and we'd have only a fighting chance of seeing the mountains through the clouds and rain. But with Omi along we felt lucky, and we were. Standing in the blunt bow of the ferry, we smiled at the freshness of the mild sea air, at the clearings of blue sky spreading between the clouds over the distant mountains.

We pulled into the ferry slip at Bremerton. Our car, first aboard the ferry, would be the first off. Was I nervous? A little tense, perhaps. Just want to be sure that damn brake is disengaged. The apron of the ferry, overlapping the landing stage, pointed up at an acute angle. I stepped on the accelerator, wrenched the hand brake off and roared slowly forward. Too fast, even so? I must have thought so, for my foot pressed the brake—much stronger, more like a hair trigger than the brakes I was used to—the car stopped with a jerk, Omi and M. were hurled forward in unison, I panicked, clutched what I thought was the hand brake and instead got the lever that unhooked the hood, which rose majestically like a hippo yawning, blotting out our view

through the windshield. Friendly men sprang from
nowhere to my aid, pressed the hood back into
place, waved me on with grins. With a red and
sweating face, I drove off the ferry. Omi and M.
were whooping and yelling with laughter.

The road soon brought us out on the coast, the
mountains of the Olympic range on our left, dodg-
ing in and out of clouds, and across the wide Juan
de Fuca Strait the gray, hilly shoreline of British
Columbia. Midafternoon brought us to the sparse
main street of Port Angeles, where we were to
spend our first night in a motel. The A.A.A. people had recommended the Flagstone, so that's where
we went.

I had never seen the inside of a motel, and the
chief impression their exteriors had made on me
was of bareness, drabness, the kind of mass-pro-
duced look of dwellings in company towns. This
one didn't seem so bad. We drove into a small
courtyard of numbered doorways, where one or
two cars were already parked. A sign over the door
nearest the street was marked "Office."

"Hello," says the man behind the desk. That's
the invariable greeting in this part of the world,
and it fits the mood of the country. He shows you
the available rooms and gives you the keys, you sign
your name and pay—in advance, in case you might
be leaving at two o'clock in the morning. Prices
vary: I think we paid as little as five dollars a room
and as much as twelve. For that you get a double
room, comfortably and often beautifully furnished,

and a private bathroom, all spotlessly clean, well heated or air-conditioned, and usually a television set (which often didn't work) as well. Some of our motels had a restaurant on the premises; more often there was a café nearby. Only once, on a Sunday morning, did we have difficulty finding a place where we could get breakfast; that time we had to drive thirty-five miles for it. But motels in such remote spots generally include kitchenettes in their cabins, and travelers can cook their own meals, if they have the wherewithal. And in that case the kitchenette is likely to contain an electric icebox, which gives you ice for your drinks; otherwise you ask for ice at the office or help yourself from one of the motel's communal ice bins.

In the course of our trip we became connoisseurs of motels. Some of them stick out in my memory like green oases: Kalaloch, Washington; Hon-dah, Arizona; Destin, Florida. These were all exceptional in being far enough from a main road so that you didn't get the whish-whish-whish of passing cars or the roar of trucks all night long. There were two things about motels that remained a mystery to us: where did their decorators learn such good taste, and why didn't they have sense enough to get farther away from the road? True, the traffic is their bread and butter, but why should they have to serve it butter side down?

Our rooms at the Port Angeles motel had reproductions of Utrillos on the walls, and the glass tumblers in the bathroom were wrapped in sanitized cellophane. Both these facts impressed M. favorably—she has a fellow feeling for Utrillo and a horror of dirt. Also she had been much cheered, as we passed the local drive-in theater, by the triple feature advertised for Fri., Sat., Sun.:

> *THE BLOB*
> *THE HANGMAN*
> *I MARRIED A MONSTER*

Next morning I was having breakfast at Aggie's Café when Omi came in.

"What's that you're eating?" she said. "It looks delicious."

"That, my dear Omi, is a butterhorn. Not to be confused with a thunder-egg."

"They sound exciting. What are they?"

"I think a thunder-egg is a little piece of meteorite found in these parts and polished up for the tourist trade. But a butterhorn, as you see, is what effete Easterners might call a coffee cake. Try one."

"I believe I will."

M. joined us a little later. The sun was out, and we all felt hopeful. I felt so hopeful that I ordered another butterhorn. Outcries from the ladies, references to calorie content and unrestrained American eating habits. Did I want to end up looking like the usual overweight American male, all chins and belly? The waitress said, "They're trying to make you feel guilty. Don't you let them."

"What exactly is a rain forest?" said Omi.

Neither M. nor I knew exactly, but we discussed the matter and decided that it must be (a) primeval, (b) attractive to rain, (c) rare. The one we were driving through now seemed to fill that bill. The trees, though not many of them were tremendously large, looked old; it was not raining at the moment, but the rank undergrowth, the whole forest, was saturated with damp, and there were puddles in the road.

We drove slowly, so as not to miss anything, and also because of the potholes, and after a while it got rather depressing.

"It's very beautiful, but I don't think I'd like to *live* in a rain forest," said Omi.

"But how beautiful it is," I said.

"Ah."

"I wish I could really *see* it."

"You're looking at it," said M.

"But not seeing it properly. I don't know one tree from another, so how can I? And they can't all be pines."

The same day we drove up a mountain road, the only one that's open at this season, to get a look at the whole Olympic National Park. The road ended in twenty-five miles, but by then we were six thousand feet up, above timber line, and the view was immense: a silent wilderness of forest-covered hills and snow-capped mountains, as far as the eye could reach. By the side of the road there was a stone restaurant, shut for the season. No temples; no other sign of man, not even a forest ranger's lookout that we could see.

"It's *big*," said Omi.

M. wanted to know how big, and which one was Mt. Olympus. Omi refrained from guessing, while M. and I aired our theories. M. wished we had a guidebook. We had tried several times to get one and were always told either that such a thing didn't exist or that it was out of print. I had picked up a "tour book" from the Automobile Association which was useful on motels but not much good on anything else.

M. had been studying a map. "Some of these names," she said. "Wonderful. Just listen to this: Humptulips. Shine. Potlatch. And these: Dabob, Sequim, Waatch, Pysht."

"They sound as if they'd just missed."

"Where do you suppose they came from?"

"Rugged pioneers trying to pronounce rugged Indian."

"Oh, here are some beauties," cried M. "Three rivers, side by side: Dosewallips, Duckabush, and Hamma Hamma."

...

It was obviously going to rain any minute. I had warned Omi and M. that it rained most of the time

in this country, and they are both great sun lovers;
but the land was so beautiful and their spirits were
so high that they didn't mind.

"Let it rain," said Omi. Whereupon it began to
rain almost immediately.

At Kalaloch (pronounced K'*lay*-lock, though M.
and Omi could never get it quite right), we holed
up for three days at an almost-deserted lodge, overlooking the enormous gray Pacific.

Does the Pacific—all you can see of it from the
land—actually look bigger than, say, Lake Baikal?
(M. points out that I've never seen Lake Baikal.)
All right, bigger than the Mediterranean, or Lake
Superior? Yes, it does, though perhaps that's because you know it's the greatest of all oceans. Not
entirely, however; the coast has something to do
with it, and this wild and empty shore matches the
immensity of the sea.

Under the gray, rain-heavy sky, M. and I walked
along the deserted beach, which stretched out north
and south, apparently forever. The fine white sand
was colorless in that silver light. Instead of dunes,
a continuous low bluff cut off our view on the land-
ward side; all we could see, inland, were the scrubby
fringes of forest. The only sound was the whisper
and tiny crash of the waves. M. said it looked like
the beginning of the world. It did; yet if so, the
world must have been going for some time before
that—long enough to pile up these endless wind-
rows of dead trees, stripped and polished by sea,
wind and sand to dull silver and old bone. Wher-

ever we got a glimpse of this coast we saw that beach boneyard, mile after mile of it. No one seemed to notice it; no one bothered to glean it.

An inlet, half choked with a jumble of branches and logs, wound between our lodge and the beach, a wild foreground to the larger wildness of the sea. Our landlady told us that a pair of otters often came there to play. We watched for them every day, but never caught sight of them.

The lodge at Kalaloch, where we spent three happy days, was owned and managed by a middle-aged couple named Becker. Mrs. Becker, we all agreed, was a life enhancer, and one of the most encouraging women you could hope to find anywhere. She was plain, bespectacled, sensible and friendly: she liked the human race, without wanting to be intimate with it. She worked from dawn to dark, with loud, cheerful cries—not to keep her spirits up, but because that was her nature. Even though it was off season and we were almost the only overnight visitors, she had a lot of work to get through. It would have been better done if she had been able to do it all herself, but it was too much for her. Her only visible helpers were a part-time waitress, her daughter (home from college for the weekend), and two gum-chewing teen-aged girls in blue jeans and pony-tailed hair who came in for an hour or so to make beds and flick a duster—but mostly just to chatter.

Mrs. Becker's domain included six cottages and the lodge itself (eight bedrooms and baths, an upstairs bar, dining room and sandwich counter). Luckily Mr. Becker, a tall, quiet man dressed invariably in work clothes, was gadget-minded. With laconic pride he showed us his ice-making machine, which turned out sheets of ice cubes the size of a thumbnail, and explained the workings of the electric signaling system which put him and Mrs. Becker in touch with each other in whatever far-apart rooms they happened to be.

By European standards, the Beckers were rich: the value of their property, translated into foreign currency, would have put them into the class of comfortable idlers, and some of its amenities could hardly have been matched by any luxury hotel in Europe; and yet both of them worked like peasants to keep their place going.

▰▰▰

M. thought the vast silence of this Pacific Northwest was reflected in the quiet behavior and talk of its inhabitants; for the first time she stopped complaining about people's voices. She could hardly wait to see the Indians, who she was sure would be a minor copy of the scenery. While we were staying at the lodge in Kalaloch one or two Indians came in for a cup of coffee, but they looked like anybody else, except for their darker faces and lank black hair. M. refused to take them as representative; she wanted to see them on their own reservation.

The big Quinault reservation was only a few

miles south, and our road took us through it. The first settlement we saw was so dingily uninviting and so unlike what M. thought it should be that we didn't stop. It was a small shantytown, where a few emaciated dogs slunk after us and barked, and the only Indians we saw were some staring children, like little dark dolls, a fat old woman, and two men in black hats tinkering with a broken-down car. Also tin cans and rusty junk. Later that day we drove a few miles out of our way to see the chief settlement, Moclips. It was bigger, and there were more Indians. Also more junk.

We stopped for coffee at a resort motel high on a bluff, with a sparkling view of the sea and the rocky coast. A sign just inside the door read: "The opinions of the husband in this house are not necessarily those of the management." On the subject of Indians, however, they seemed to feel the same way. The couple who owned the place joined us for coffee and talked about Indians with affection and enthusiasm. But they didn't like what was happening to their Indians. According to them, the big lumber companies were stealing their reservation right out from under them. At birth, every Indian child in the Quinault tribe is allotted eighty acres of timberland—worth at least a thousand dollars an acre, our informants said. The Indians are also allowed to fish all year and there is no closed season for them on game. But they want cash, in order to buy cars and other glorious toys. When these break down or wear out, the Indians simply pile them up outside their houses, as a sign of prestige and affluence. To get cash they sell their timber rights; they have even taken to selling their land as well. The timber companies now own half the reservation; when three quarters of the land is gone the reservation by law will be liquidated.

6

Paradise Overrun

In Seaside, Oregon, we stayed in our first motel with a swimming pool. For breakfast we went down the street to a gleaming little box of a café ("We Serve Breakfast All Day"). Not more than ten people could have crowded in, but the owner proudly told us he had sixteen thousand dollars' worth of the most modern equipment, including an electronic oven. I said I'd have a boiled egg. No, he couldn't boil an egg; no equipment for that.

...

It was still the same mild, damp, sea-laden air, but once we were across the broad, fjordlike mouth of the Columbia River, the land changed. Washington's forests had given way to the meadowland of Oregon. This part of the state looked a little too civilized.

The city of Portland, where we spent a night, did not appeal to us. Next day we drove along the Columbia River to the famous Bonneville Dam, whose dual function is to make electric power and help the homing salmon to their spawning grounds. It was the fish ladder rather than the giant turbines that we wanted to see. But our timing was unlucky —we were too early for the salmon. All we saw were a few eels, their sucker mouths clinging grimly to a temporary perch against the weight of the pouring water.

···

It was smorgasbord night, the waiter told us— just help ourselves from the big table over there. For once the food was delicious. We had been lucky to find this restaurant in a town as small as Ashland. But it was a college town, which might account for the foreign bill of fare and the presence at a nearby table of half a dozen people, apparently young professors and their wives having an evening out. They were making a lively time of it, drinking and flirting. At one end of the table a woman who seemed older than the others kept patting and fondling the not very receptive man next to her. This lady was the first to leave, amid cries of regret that rang with a certain note of relief; her departure brought a marked lessening of tension and a burst of shop talk. M. was fascinated, and jotted down bits of it in her notebook.

"There's never been an unselfish act in history."

"I don't believe that. Never! I'd slit my throat if I believed that."

"I'm a flack—but I admit it."

"What's he doing? Training juvenile delinquents?"

"I'm very weary of reformers. Got no faith in the reformation of the human race—waste of time. So many bad, so many good, it doesn't matter what you do. If you cure cancer, you can get something else."

His wife says, "You *promised* no arguments."

"Ah, this is fun!"

"We've already passed Aldous Huxley's *Brave New World* by a hundred years."

"You unhappy? I can stop that. Take the new medicines."

"This rule of the mechanical over humanity is impossible."

"I'm inept, so I'm afraid of making them all a part of the group."

"Machines are controlling my life."

"I'm scared of the machines."

Most motels supply postcards and little brochures advertising local shops, etc., but no magazines or newspapers. In one motel in southern Oregon, however, I found a *Hospitality Guide to the Rogue Valley*, which contained some livelier bits

—e.g., "Auto seat belts are vital to public safety. They keep the drivers from leaving the scene of the accident."

...

Now we're encamped beside the Rogue River, a full, racing, shallow stream, rushing over cobbly stones and boulders, and packed (they say) with fish called steelheads. Our cottage, rented for two nights, stands with other cottages (all empty) on the sandy verge of the river, but too near the truck-infested road. For the past eight days we've driven from one motel to another, always being sure of finding one—from Seattle along the Pacific coast to Portland, then up the Columbia River for a bit, and south through central Oregon.

Hood River, Rhododendron, Ashland, Trail (where we are now): those have been our stopping places. We avoid motels in towns when we can. So far, for aggressive charmlessness I think we'd give the palm to Klamath Falls. Mr. K. says Russia will be the same in another seven years, God help us.

It's pleasant driving, except for these towns, or on the superhighways; the roads are good, they run straight for miles, and there's very little traffic at this time of year. You just sit back and steer, and before you know it you're coasting along at seventy-five. And the land is beautiful: a variable old wild country. Great snow mountains, gorges of volcanic rock, deep dripping forests and mountain streams, then barren plateau of rock and wasteland. Indian country. Just ahead of us is California and the giant sequoias, the redwood trees that are older than the nation and as tall as skyscrapers.

▀▀▀

Yes, they are. For more than two hundred miles—not continuous, though once they may have been—they stand incredibly straight and tall, in great shadowed groves. They are much more alive than skyscrapers, more like patient and noble elephants waiting to be murdered. And they are being murdered. The Redwood Highway, down which we have come, is thunderous and risky with logging trucks carrying out the corpses. Soon, I suppose, the redwoods will be as extinct as the bison, a few last specimens preserved as museum pieces.

People can now buy tracts along the roadway and mark them as memorials to some departed member of their family—impressive monuments to some pretty odd names. We're beginning to hate the lumber companies the way elephant lovers hate ivory hunters; they both have the same attitude: kill for profit.

▀▀▀

"We're supposed to be intelligent people," said Omi, "but what do we say when we look at something as beautiful as this? We just say, 'Look at it! *Look!*'"

"Or we quote something," I said. " 'My heart leaps up when I behold . . .' "

"We only make the same noises everybody else does," said M. "There *isn't* anything adequate to say."

...

"By 1936," I said, "according to the *Encyclopae-dia Britannica*, the United States was cutting about twice as much timber as it was growing each year."

"But now we've learned that it pays to plant."

"Do you know how old some of these redwoods are—or were? Two thousand years."

...

Omi was tired that night and went to bed early. M. and I drove for twenty miles along the dark, forest-lined road, looking for a place to eat. It was Sunday, and the few cafés we passed were all closed. Finally we saw a lighted sign, "Cocktail Lounge," and went in. It was a stone building, of modern design; the bar was lined from floor to ceiling with redwood. There were a dozen men in the bar (no women), all dressed in lumbermen's heavy clothes. They stared at us warily, with not-quite hostility, glancing self-conscious looks at M. Nobody said hello.

What about that generous, openhearted American way with strangers? Well, strangers, yes, but they mustn't look or act too strange, they mustn't be *foreigners.* Perhaps we seemed foreign to them. M.'s accent sometimes got her mistaken for a Canadian, and when she was asked where she lived and she said, "London—no, not Ontario, England," that was always the end of the conversation. Nobody had the slightest interest in London, England; or perhaps it was simply too outlandish an idea, an American—or anybody—living that far away.

No, said the barkeep, no sandwiches, nothing to eat. Not even potato chips? No, nothing. It was seven o'clock; everybody but us had had his supper hours before, and now they were all drinking beer. M. and I had whiskey. After a couple of drinks we got talking to a young lumber surveyor who had come West to make some money. He wasn't worried about the destruction of the redwoods. The big lumber companies, he said, aren't as bad as they used to be; they're getting "conservation-minded" because they see it pays in the long run. "And they're all earning a living," he said with a grin.

The barkeep said, "Oh, they'll find timber on the moon—or plastics without wood or something. Too many people, that's the trouble. We need more cars to kill more people."

There was a big picture window at the back of the bar, and the light shone out on the trunks of two redwood trees; their tops went far up into the shadows. M. pointed to them and said,

"Don't you think they're beautiful?"

"That big one's worth ten to fifteen thousand

dollars. If you had ten to fifteen thousand dollars standing in your back yard, would you just leave it set there for scenery?"

"Why do people always want more money?"

"They gotta make more money. *Nobody* ever has enough money in the United States."

"But what *for?*"

"So they can buy a Cadillac and impress people."

▚▚▚

From M.'s notes:

"The natural world out here is a splendor. All else not up to it. The people here don't own, cherish, protect, with a view to eternity; they exploit, and, via advertising, are completely, ludicrously exploited.

"The motel bathrooms are lovely. I'll settle for the landscape and the bathrooms."

▚▚▚

We had all been in San Francisco before, but none of us had ever arrived there from the north, as we were coming now. It is the most exciting approach to any city I know. As Route 101 swings through San Rafael and begins the long rise to the still distant promontory that hinges the Golden Gate, you feel a mounting suspense, a promise of something tremendous soon to be seen. The road itself heightens this expectation; it must be one of the finest express highways in our modern world, a wide concrete ribbon poured cunningly into the contours of the hills, and always rising. This characteristic monument to our day would be an astonishment to men of earlier times. Our seventy miles an hour, a gentle hum, seems to suspend us in space while the brown hills on either side swell toward us and drift past; our convoying traffic is going equally fast.

As the road winds higher and the accompanying cars grow denser around us, it is impossible not to feel that we are nearing some great sight, just over the next brow. The heaven-declared edge of the continent, a dawn-like ocean, another glimpse of that "newness of life"?

And there at last it leaps into view: the far sweep of the great bay and its attendant mountains, the narrow passage of the Golden Gate and, rising tier on tier across the water, the white, island-like city. Now I have seen it—there are "thy templed hills."

7

Beatniks and Credit Cards

San Francisco is a beauty; I'd forgotten how great a beauty. Not only by contrast with other American towns and cities, but a beauty in its own right. San Francisco has, as they say, "an air about it"— the conscious and confident air of a city that is set on a hill and cannot be hid. San Franciscans do not consider themselves provincial but cosmopolitan, and this feeling has some basis in fact. Their self-sufficiency is not like the salesman's pitch of the Los Angelenos or the Texans' big brag.

Like all cities that have not begun to die, San Francisco is expanding; but by the good fortune that its site was a promontory, the city is strictly defined by its near-island limits and can expand only in one direction, down the peninsula—and South San Francisco is mercifully out of sight. Perhaps because it was mostly built—or rebuilt—at the same time, the city's streets hang together in a non-American, almost European way. M., who is convinced that all American cities allow garbage cans to clutter their sidewalks and trash and old newspapers to clog their gutters, was immediately impressed by the *cleanness* of San Francisco. An amused inhabitant later told her that most of the credit should go to the sea breeze, a daily scavenger, and the rain, which scours the steep streets more thoroughly than a housewife.

▰▰▰

M. was still fierce for fact finding, and made arrangements to attend a murder trial and a juvenile court. Omi had some friends at Berkeley whom she said she would like to see. I wanted to find an old friend who worked on a local newspaper and who could be guaranteed not to burden me with any facts; besides, we had a lot of private gossip to catch up on. It took quite a while to reach him; I landed him at last through another friend at the Pacific Union Club, and we went off for the evening.

We ended up at a favorite bar of his, where he was well known; he introduced me to the barkeep and the proprietor as "my oldest friend and a very great man." Having repeated this introduction several times, he said he didn't feel well, excused himself and went home. I stayed on and had another drink, but of course neither the barkeep nor the proprietor would so much as give me the time of day.

Omi announced that she would have to leave us for a week—some civic affair in St. Louis that she absolutely had to be there for—but that she would rejoin us in Los Angeles. Before she left, we had an evening on the town, guided by my friend the newspaperman. Although he said no San Franciscan ever went there, only tourists, I wanted to start at the Top of the Mark; neither Omi nor M. had seen it, and I remembered the view at dusk, after several drinks and with Hawaiian music in the background, as one of the great sights. And it was just as I remembered it. We arrived early enough to get a table at a window looking west and watched the glow fade out of the sky over the Golden Gate, while the lights of the city below us came twinkling on, and even Alcatraz looked like a dark jewel. As the room filled up, the noise of people talking was so loud you couldn't have heard the music if there had been any, but otherwise everything was the way I wanted it to be, and Omi and M. were pleased and impressed.

We should have left it at that and never gone back. A few evenings later we tried it again: the sunset was of inferior quality and the view not nearly so spectacular, and it took forever to get a drink.

On our night out with Omi, my newspaper friend took us after dinner to a bar on the waterfront known as Pier 23. It was an old-fashioned kind of saloon, with framed photographs on the walls. One of the photographs showed a small man with a mediocre face and his mouth wide open, like an O. That was the proprietor, a man named Havelock Jerome, and he was singing. He never sang unless he was drunk, and he was so awful it was funny, or anyhow people liked it and tried to get him drunk so he would sing. At this point Mr. Jerome himself appeared and was introduced to us. He was nowhere near drunk and said modestly that he had no voice. But the sight of Omi, who really has an effect on people, brought out all the chivalrous grandiloquence of his nature. He bowed, kissed her on the cheek and said, "May I reiterate that I love you?"

▄▄▄

When we had put Omi on her bus for the plane, M. and I went on our separate rounds, but we usually met in the evenings. Once we went to a night club which was famous as the place where the great Mort Sahl got his start, but we didn't know that; we went because we liked the name, "the hungry i." The headliner of the show there was billed as "Professor Irwin Corey, the World's Foremost Authority." He was quite funny, especially at first, when he didn't say a word.

M. and I also took a look at the beatniks. We were told that Grant Avenue was the place. The Coexistence Bagel Shop turned out to be a squalid little beer hall that gave off a strong counterfeit smell. The crowd was young, but most of them looked more like bums than beatniks. The art galleries and the bookshops, open till a late hour, were more like it. The pictures varied from commercial fourth-rate to noncommercial third-rate, and there were few buyers. The bookshops were not doing much better, but M. was favorably impressed by the fact that they sold only paperbacks, and by the quality and the variety of the books themselves. Still, she thought they weren't cheap enough; some of them were as much as $2.50. In the first one we entered, a man was sitting at a table eating a plate of spaghetti with chopsticks, and didn't even glance up as we came in. He had a sparse beatnik beard and looked half Chinese, half Negro.

M. met a young doctor whose hobby was beatniks, and one evening he took us to a cellar where poets recited their stuff to the accompaniment of a jazz band. The poet that night was a lank-haired girl. She chanted her lines in a high monotone, and the band sometimes drowned her out, but not often enough.

▚▚▚

M. met a Chinese social worker.

"Do you know what he told me today? He said that before the war there were no Chinese delinquents in San Francisco."

"I suppose they stayed home and honored their fathers and mothers."

"Exactly. But now they're getting assimilated to the American way of life."

"Which includes juvenile delinquency?"

"That's it. And it worries him."

▄▄▄

One of the features in a San Francisco paper is a column in which a reporter puts the same question to passers-by on a street corner and prints their answers, with their names, photographs and addresses. This day's question was: "Is it all right for celebrities to live on a different moral level?"

The answer from Jim Maniscalco, student: "Everyone should have the same morals. Like Johnny Mathis is my favorite singer, but he should be clean. Sometimes you can't help it if you get into trouble, like with women, but you should stay out of it if you can."

▄▄▄

We had heard about the wonderful invention of credit cards, and seen jokes about them in *The New Yorker*. They sounded like just the ticket for this trip. A friend in New York told us we should get two: American Express and the Diners' Club. With those two, he said, you could charge anything, with the possible exception of an abortion, anywhere in America. As we understood it, we could sign for all our bills, which would be paid by American Express; once a month we would get an

itemized bill from that company, and this neat
bookkeeping would greatly simplify our expense
account. So we duly applied for the cards and
eventually got them.

But of course that's not the way it works at all.
In the first place, credit cards are not accepted
"everywhere"—far from it. You can't sign for a
plane ticket unless you have *another* credit card
specially for air travel. You can sign for a railroad
ticket, but only if you go to an office of the American Express Company to get it, and you will then
be charged an additional fee ($1.50, as I remem-
ber). Your credit card is good only at the hotels,
motels, shops and restaurants that belong to the
system, and at least half the time they are not the
ones you want. In restaurants, particularly, when
I proffered my credit card I often got the impression that it was acceptable but not welcomed, that
cash would have been preferred. And why not?
Whenever these places give you a meal on credit
they have to pay a commission of seven per cent to
the company that issued the card, and in the case of
a small restaurant that commission might eat up
most of the profit.

As for American Express paying the bills and
then sending you an itemized accounting, that
wasn't so either. Half the time the bill came direct
to me, which at first confused and then annoyed
me. And when I say "direct," I don't quite mean
that. When I applied for credit cards I had to give
my home address as London, England; but I ex-

plained that in order to save both the company and me time and trouble, I wanted the bills sent care of Omi in St. Louis. Otherwise I foresaw the bills going slowly across the Atlantic to London and then being sent slowly back across the Atlantic again to try to find me somewhere in America. As it turned out, not much time was saved by my forethought, and no trouble.

The bills arrived so tardily that, although we were back in London before Christmas, some were still coming in at the end of February. Since neither side thought the other worthy of air mail, I often got several bills in succession for the same charge and paid some of them twice over. One hotel in Washington, D.C., when I discovered my mistake and wrote to ask for my money back, handsomely refunded my overpayment and explained that no doubt they would have discovered the error themselves when their accounts were overhauled at the end of the year.

In the same way I overpaid American Express by $356.41, and had a hell of a time getting my money back. I suppose their case was that, since I had been issued a credit card that was good for a year, they weren't going to close their books on me till the year was up. My case was that I'd wanted the credit card for only a few months, that my trip was now over and I never wanted to see the damn thing again, and could I please have my money back? I suppose the negotiations might have gone on until my unwanted credit card expired. If, indeed, you can call them negotiations. On my side I would write a clear, insistent, not too emotional letter, explaining the facts and asking for my money; on their side, they would reply with another fully automated, mysteriously perforated card which looked like a bill but on closer inspection turned out to be a third or fourth statement that my account was credited with $356.41.

This affair threatened to outlast the treaty talks at Panmunjom, and seemed as hopeless, until I got the happy idea of getting in touch with somebody on their side who wasn't a machine. I telephoned to the London office of American Express to try to find that human being, and after telling my story several times I was at last switched to the right man, a Mr. Pyle. He understood, he sympathized, he assured me that he would write a hot letter and get some action. I told him that letters were hopeless, he was up against Frankenstein's monster. He said, "Leave it to me." What else could I do?

That was early in April. In the middle of May I actually received a check for $356.41 from American Express. Meantime one more automated and perforated card had arrived, stating that my credit was now $365.62—the ante had been raised another nine dollars. I reported these facts to Mr. Pyle and said I was well satisfied with his triumph, and let's forget the extra nine dollars. Not he; by this time his blood was up, and he said again, "Leave it to me." As far as I know, he's still in there, fighting those machines.

So M. and I don't think much of credit cards.

▀▀▀

I took a train to Palo Alto, to look up a freshman at Stanford, the son of an old friend. He was at a class, but his roommate drew me a map of the campus so that I could wander about without getting lost. On the back of the paper were some notes he had made, perhaps in a lecture: "Competition as a kind of dependence. Close competition destructive?" I should like to have heard more about that.

8

Out of This World

M.'s feeling about trains is much the same as mine about planes: she thinks them obsolete, uncomfortable and unsafe. It was therefore a considerable concession when she agreed to take a train to Los Angeles. To cheer her up I pointed out that the plane trip would have been very costly with all our overweight, and that the Lark was probably the finest train left in America. I said she'd enjoy the overnight journey and find it all too short.

She didn't, however. She objected to the roadbed, the food in the diner and the narrow limits of her compartment; and next morning she said she hadn't slept a wink all night, how could she, being hurled about in her bunk like that? Not to speak of the appalling noise.

Nevertheless, the Lark got us to Los Angeles on

time and, from M.'s point of view, very early in the morning. (I got up for breakfast in the diner and had the first good cup of coffee I'd tasted in the West.) M. liked the Spanish-mission look of the Southern Pacific station, with its palms and patios, and the casual California-style clothes and manner of the strolling crowds, a pleasant contrast to the bawl and bustle of stations in the East. While she had her breakfast in the coffee shop I went to the Hertz office, overlooking the station patio, to sign for our next car. It was waiting for us, a silver-gray Chevrolet convertible. I discovered the right knob to pull to get the top down, and off we drove to the Mojave Desert.

That morning we passed a lot of gas stations and a military reservation—warning signs and miles of barbed wire—but saw nothing remotely like the peace and emptiness of the desert that had been described to us. The owner of the roadside restaurant where we stopped for lunch was sympathetic and helpful; he admitted that the Mojave Desert was not what it used to be but said there were still some good spots in it. He strongly recommended a motel about a hundred miles away.

"It's out of this world," he said.

That was just what we wanted, we replied, and we thanked him warmly. We found it with no trouble; indeed, it would have been hard to miss—an oversize supermotel with all the worst features of a country club, and loud signs proclaiming itself a shrine of good fellowship, a temple of togetherness. The circular courtyard was already, in mid-afternoon, more than half filled with cars. We looked at each other without speaking and drove on.

A few miles further we turned up a side road which gave some promise of leading us to the real desert, and it did. Ten miles down the road, topping a low hill, we found the kind of motel we had been looking for. The view from our bedroom windows was immense: enormous empty desert falling away to the unseen Mojave River and then slowly rising again to the horizon; to the left a sweep of distant mountains; and not another human habitation in sight. The couple who ran the motel ("Call us Fran and Bill") were young and friendly, and full of enthusiasm about the region. Only two other people were staying there: an elderly couple from Catalina.

M. was ecstatic over this isolated haven. Disillusion began at dusk: as the sunset faded, lights went on all over the desert. Far from being alone in an empty land, we were surrounded, hemmed in by "developments." Nor had we escaped a more active togetherness; when we went into the dining room for dinner only one table was laid, and for six. M. didn't like that a bit, but she bore up well. Even when Bill grew dogmatic on politics and revealed himself as a strong supporter of Nixon, she held her hand and turned the conversation to Catalina Island. The elderly couple replied rather guardedly to her questions. From what they said it appeared that Catalina, the private property of the Wrigley chewing-gum family, has much in common with a feudal estate. Whether they thought the perquisites of this vassalage outweighed the disadvantages we couldn't make out. They traveled a good deal, they said—were *they* changing the subject too?—but had never been out of the West, and were mildly surprised that anybody should want to go elsewhere. What did the rest of the country have, or Europe, that couldn't be found here, except a few old cathedrals?

Next day we walked down to the Mojave River —only a couple of miles, Bill told us, but we went a good deal further than that without finding any river, though I think we must have crossed its dry bed. That walk finished the Mojave Desert for M. We hadn't gone more than fifty yards before we stumbled on the first beer can; they were all over the place, also scraps of old newspaper and other artifacts.

Before we left, Bill said that it wasn't too late to buy land hereabouts, but we'd better act fast, real-estate values were booming.

▄▄▄

We got our first solid mouthful of Los Angeles driving in by the San Bernardino Freeway. I belong to the generation that was born before cars were in common use, and when I was a boy we were often taken out "for a spin," for pleasure. I can't imagine anyone nowadays driving anywhere near

Los Angeles for pleasure. "For kicks," yes, if you're a desperate hot-rodder or a drunken actor. It was a relief to turn in the car, though that meant taking taxis, at an average of five dollars a trip.

After we'd unpacked, M. discovered by the lettering on the bathmat that our hotel was one of the Schine chain, owned by the father of one of that ill-famed pair, Cohn and Schine, who had been Joe McCarthy's private bloodhounds. We hated to add even a few dollars to the fortunes of this un-American, but decided it was too much trouble to move for the short time we would be here.

▲▲▲

One feature that struck my eye in the Los Angeles newspapers—which are not very interesting and are deprecated even by Los Angelenos as not being the best in the world—was the weather report. "No smog today," or "Slight smog."

The first time I visited the city, smog had not yet been invented; it's the bad breath that bespeaks Los Angeles' monstrous glandular growth.

▲▲▲

I said to M., "I just spent forty-five cents for a small orange juice at that clip-joint soda fountain across the street."

"It doesn't surprise me."

"And a thought came to me, not about the orange juice but about Los Angeles as a whole. I wanted to say something firm but just, the kind of pronouncement Gibbon might have made when he wasn't prejudiced."

"Yes?"

"Here it is: 'Except in a moment of utter dejection no one would seriously contend that Los Angeles exemplifies, in any of its aspects, the best that man can do.' "

"Gibbon would have been proud of you."

▴▴▴

I knew one Hollywood character and M. knew another. First we went to lunch with mine. We met him at his office on the Supercolossal Pictures lot. His office was in a bungalow, with his name on a brass plate on the front door: Sam Hartford. Sam and I are very old friends, by Hollywood standards. We first met about ten years ago, and since then I suppose I've seen him half a dozen times, mostly in night clubs. In the words of an advertising salesman I used to know (who later became a college president), "You'd love him. He's the sweetest fellow in the picture business."

Sam fell upon us with outstretched arms and low cries of happiness; within three minutes he was calling M. by her first name or simply "darling." I could see that M. thought Sam a wonderfully pure example of Hollywood. And as far as I know, he is. I haven't met many of Hollywood's temporary tycoons, but none I have seen or heard about strikes such a clear note of phoniness as Sam. There is something innocent, or at least old-boyishly engaging, about his barefaced imitation of an open-hearted Simple Simon. A child could see through it. He has had "screen credits" as writer of some films that were successful and also pretty good, but I don't remember ever seeing his name alone; he always had a partner. I sometimes wondered how much of a writer Sam actually was. Anyhow, he had gone up in the world; he was now, he told us, a producer as well. "I'm wearing two hats," he said happily.

He started to tell us about the fearless and hard-hitting picture he was getting ready, but a young assistant came in to remind him of an urgent matter, and his phone rang. I had a feeling that he welcomed these interruptions, that in a sense he needed them. The telephone call was from Dallas, from someone whom Sam jovially hailed as "General!" —making it sound like "Old horse thief!"—and railed at for being so hard to find. Now that he had been found, Sam was trying to arrange a meeting, purpose undisclosed. I guessed duck shooting. While this conversation was going on, M. and I stared at everything—the hunting prints on the wall, the thick green carpet on the floor, the low-lying leather chairs and couch, the magazine table (*Life, Holiday, The New Yorker, Illustrated London News*)—but avoided looking at each other.

No sooner had Sam hung up and excused himself and begun to tell us what a lovely fellow the General was than the phone rang again. Sam answered it, and an expression of sophisticated delight

erased the boyish candor from his face. This time
the conversation was sufficiently obvious: Sam was
going on a yachting weekend with some pals—and
girls; he and his friend were discussing where and
when to meet.

Out of deference to M., Sam felt it necessary to
explain that he was no longer married; he referred
to his former wife with vague but bitter wistful-
ness. I remembered meeting her on my last visit to
Hollywood. Sam had driven me to his house in his
new M.G. and proudly presented his wife—she
seemed harder than Sam, equally synthetic, and
much prettier—and a half-grown son. It was not
clear whether the boy was Sam's own son or his
wife's by an earlier marriage. I had heard without
surprise that he and his wife had parted. At our
only meeting Sam had exhibited her, the boy and
the M.G. in the same self-congratulatory style, as
if they were all interchangeable parts in a design
for gracious living.

M. has a friend who has made a fortune out of
Hollywood, though he refuses to live there. He
sells the screen rights to most of his novels and
some of his stories and picks up other thousands by
working over other people's scripts. She mentioned his name and asked Sam if he knew him.

Sam's mobile face took on a mask of bitterness
and he laughed harshly. "He's a grand fellow. I'm
devoted to him. Of course, he could be arrested for
grand larceny. What film did he ever make? He
comes out here and sells a story for a pile of money.

Do they ever make the picture? If they do, it's a flop. Him a writer for the movies—that's a laugh. But he's got an attitude, so he gets away with murder. I love him, he's great."

We went to the commissary for lunch, passing through the noisy and crowded cafeteria where the ordinary mortals ate to the noisy and crowded but smaller room reserved for executives and other big shots. Sam explained that the hierarchic order applied here too: only the top executives sat at the row of tables nearest the window; the second row, where we were, was the preserve of the producers, and so on down. The writers, who just barely had the right of entry, were huddled at the last table, next to the door.

Lunch was a series of gay interruptions. From the front row, heavy hard-faced men with bald heads or thinning gray hair, Sam's cheery greetings drew only nods, grunts or a curt wave of the hand; but from the tables behind us and from the later arrivals he raised an equally hearty response, and a series of movie stars—some of them in make-up and costume—gossip writers and directors converged on our table. Each time, Sam and I would rise to our feet for a minute of bantering backchat for Sam, a manly, sincere handclasp or courtly bows for M. and me. I made a mental note to tell M. one of my theories about Hollywood: that its denizens can communicate with each other only by bodily contact—the hand on the shoulder, the squeeze of the upper arm (or, better, the knee), the two-handed handshake (almost as though you were shaking hands with yourself), lingering, long drawn out, reluctantly abandoned. Where had this touch system come from? Had it been brought to Hollywood by the Central Europeans or was it more native: the lonely anxiety, masquerading as exaggerated delight, of an American searching for his fellow, for somebody else reassuringly like himself?

In spite of these numerous introductions we finished most of our stuffed tomato and iced coffee, and then Sam said it was time to go on the set if we wanted to see a picture being made. It was a courtroom scene; the film was based on a play that was based on the Scopes trial in Dayton, Tennessee, the famous case in which William Jennings Bryan upheld the cause of fundamentalism against Clarence Darrow, arguing for the theory of evolution. Spencer Tracy was playing Darrow, Fredric March was Bryan; Gene Kelly and Florence Eldridge were other headliners in the large cast. They'd been at it since early morning, and when we got there they were having a breather while the assistant director drove home some details about the movements of the courtroom audience. Each of the stars—and the director—seemed glad to see Sam, who introduced us all around. The director called for silence, and we tiptoed off as they began to run through the scene once more. Three minutes a day of finished film, said Sam, was par for the course. That fact of Hollywood life impressed us.

It didn't hold, however, for the other set Sam took us to. Here they were shooting a "quickie" for television; only three days were allowed for making the entire film. The cast was small, four actors, and they seemed tired and bored. It was hack work they were doing, for a Grade C movie.

We said goodbye to Sam and thanked him. He waved us off as if we were his oldest and dearest friends. Perhaps we were.

▴▴▴

M.'s Hollywood character, Phil Fentriss, invited us to dinner. You could hardly say he lived on the outskirts of Los Angeles, since the whole city is outskirts; or that he lived some distance from the center, since there is no center. In any case, his house was some forty miles from our hotel, an eight-dollar taxi ride. And it was a real house, which might once have been a barn. The living room, which Fentriss also used as a workroom, was long and lofty, with windows on both sides, a raftered roof, and a big fireplace at the end.

Fentriss was a writer, too, but not the Sam Hartford type. He worked at home, and though his main job was writing for the movies, he had published one or two books as well. In Hollywood he rated as an intellectual, not to say an egghead. M. was enthusiastic about him and proud to introduce him to me.

His wife was away, but he gave us a bang-up dinner, which he himself had cooked: fried steak, baked Idaho potatoes and salad. Bourbon on the rocks beforehand, and a bottle of good California wine with dinner. Afterward, he told us, a few people would be coming in for drinks and talk. As we were finishing our coffee they all arrived together—three men and their wives. Fentriss had told us that two of the men wrote music for films and the other wrote scripts; one of the wives had been an actress, but now none of the women did anything in particular.

Only one of the wives was noticeable, and that was because she was young and recently married (or remarried, I suppose) and her husband couldn't keep his hands off her. After they'd all left, Fentriss told us that at the time of the "Hollywood Ten" that man had been blacklisted but had saved his skin by informing on other people. Had this been forgiven him? M. asked. Not so much forgiven, Fentriss said, as officially forgotten.

One of the guests, a dark, heavy-set man with thick eyeglasses, a thick European accent and a loud, bullying manner, soon made general conversation impossible. He wanted the floor and he got it. I could tell he was a musician because of the way he talked about other musicians; he said they were no good. Nobody now writing music was any good at all—fakes, plagiarists or just no talent. And the conductors! They were the boys who were really fooling the public. He sounded like Goliath strutting before the camp of the Children of Israel, hurling insults and daring anyone to come out and fight him. Unfortunately we had no David among us. When he failed to provoke a row on his chosen subject he picked another. London, he said, is a second-rate provincial town, bypassed by every-thing first-rate and inhabited exclusively by has-beens; it is of no interest to a really civilized person. He compared London unfavorably with Holly-wood. He must have been told that M. and I lived in London, and hoped we would rise to that bait. We did. When we warmed up enough to sling some intentionally rude remarks—M. much more effectively than I—he collapsed into near-geniality. It turned out that he was hoping to go to London soon for an extended visit.

Phil Fentriss told us later that this man hated Hollywood, hated his job and probably hated him-self.

▴▴▴

We heard a story in Hollywood: it was decided to link up all the computing machines in the world; by pooling their mechanical brains, it was hoped that some fundamental questions could be an-swered. The link-up was duly made, and when all was ready the President of the United States asked the first great question: "Is there a God?" For sev-eral minutes there was such silence over all the earth that the only sound was the whirring and clicking of the massed computers. Then the answer came back: "There is now."

▴▴▴

I have never understood how any Californian—
or anybody else, for that matter—could deliberately choose to live in southern California when he
might live in San Francisco. Yet a great many people obviously prefer Los Angeles. I know some. On
this visit a few of them admitted to me that it was
not choice but necessity. Los Angeles has become
such a monstrosity, even to Californians, that for
every three new arrivals two disgruntled inhabitants leave.

I said to M., "Can you understand why anyone
would want to live here?"

"*Want* to?"

"Well, put up with it."

"Lots of reasons. They don't know any better.
The climate—you can anyhow get away from the
smog weekends if you've got a car, and everyone's
got a car. The movies, if that's your line. Real estate, if thinking big makes your heart beat faster."

"Yes. El Dorado. It was always a pretty tinny
notion, and look how lousy it is when it's translated into American fact. But I know a man who
likes Los Angeles for itself. He likes its *attitude*."

"If his faculties are unimpaired, I bet he changes
his mind."

▄▄▄

The faces of Spyros Skouras, Louis B. Mayer,
Sam Goldwyn and company have never appealed
to me. There was also a man named Schenck (I
think); but my scunner against him was purely per-

sonal, as he married Norma Talmadge, with whom
I was in love as a boy. Everything I have heard and
read about these rulers of the picture industry
seems to me either ugly or sinister or both. Sam
Goldwyn, the Mrs. Malaprop or Casey Stengel of
Hollywood, might be thought an exception.
Whether from wily press-agentry or his own wily
talent he has become a kind of legendary lightning
rod for his fellow tycoons, a comforting indication
that an American can be an endearing buffoon and
a smart businessman at the same time. No doubt the
funniest Goldwynisms are as apocryphal as the say-
ings of Oxford's famous Canon Spooner. But two
anecdotes I heard about Sam Goldwyn ring reveal-
ingly true.

Frank Shields, the best-looking big-time tennis
player America has yet produced, once had a notion to become a movie actor, and Sam Goldwyn
hired him, on the strength of his profile and glorious physique—not for his fame as an athlete, of
which Goldwyn was apparently unaware. But
Shields displayed small talent for acting. He was
still a great man on the tennis courts, however, and
when he won a local tournament the news reached
Goldwyn, who next day summoned Shields to his
office.

"Schultz," he said coldly, "you can play tennis.
Act!"

The other saying I heard attributed to Sam
Goldwyn was his epitaph on his colleague Louis B.
Mayer. The reason so many people turned out for

his funeral, said Goldwyn, was that they all wanted to make sure he was dead.

▴▴▴

"You know that Shakespeare line, M., 'The expense of spirit in a waste of shame'?"

"Yes, what about it?"

"I've never really known what it means, I'm not sure I do now—as it was meant to be understood. But I think it fits Los Angeles like a hand-made glove."

"Even though you don't know what it means?"

"I don't know what Los Angeles means, either. But, as the fellow says, I tremble to think."

"And you don't think Los Angeles is typically American?"

"God, I hope not."

9

$50,000 for the View

Just before we took off for Arizona, Omi rejoined us. M. and I immediately felt more hopeful about everything.

"California, here we go."

Omi said, "I've always wanted to see the Southwest. Won't it be *wonderful!*"

In Phoenix the November sun was bright; the wind blew in gusts and swoops, counterpointing the rattles and bangs of construction and the screaming traffic that had kept us wakeful most of the night. As I leaned into the wind at an intersection, a cheerful citizen stumped past me in wrist crutches and shouted, "Get your sails up this morning!"

We did; we were anxious to get away from Phoenix. Our hired car was a Ford, salmon-pink and cream. When I went to the Hertz agency to get it, one of the two girl clerks was just going out to lunch. She picked up a movie magazine from the other girl's desk and said, "I'm going to borrow your book."

Beyond Scottsdale we found a patch of comparatively uncluttered country and a small motel, not yet open for the season, whose manager agreed to take us in for a night. We wanted the great open spaces. Where were they? M. asked the manager where we could find a really *remote* place. He said, "This is about as remote as you'll get."

"What about open country?"

"Country's a thing of the past around here."

We drove in to Scottsdale for dinner. A sign on the main street proclaimed it "the most Western town in the West." With its hitching posts and its false fronts, it looked like a movie set for a Western. M. wanted a cheap notebook and had to pay $1.02 for one that would have been dear at a quarter. The "Lulu Belle," where we had dinner, was gussied up in nineteenth-century mining-camp style; the food was excellent, and the bill would have made New Yorkers feel at home.

In spite of what the Westerners have done to it, the Western landscape inspires hope. After we came back from dinner, we stood outside the motel and looked at the sky. It was big and clear, with a wide red sunset; some jets had left long silvery vapor trails. In the distance we could see the black outlines of mountains. You could hardly hear the traffic.

"Desert air, M."

"Ah."

"Isn't it *lovely!*" said Omi.

"Except for the damn cars."

"And all this *development*."

▲▲▲

The Apache Trail sounded inviting, so we took it. And there were the first promissory glimpses of the kind of country we had hoped for: sudden sweeping vistas of desert and table-topped mountain, bare redstone canyons framing impossibly far horizons. But the road never shook civilization loose for long: the ugly little towns, the motels, the bragging billboards and the traffic.

At Miami—the Arizona town whose representative Amazons we had encountered weeks before in Seattle—we stayed overnight at the best-equipped motel we had found yet. Besides the usual amenities it had hot and cold air conditioning, TV, a telephone in each room, a heated swimming pool, an icemaking machine in the courtyard (just help yourself to all the ice you wanted), a coffee shop, a dining room and a bar. It was also one of the most expensive ($10.20 a room) and the noisiest, being bang on top of the much-traveled highway.

And next day we found the Southwest.

"Ever hear of Salt River Canyon?"

None of us ever had. Our Automobile Association tour book didn't even bother to list it under "What to See" in Arizona, and only mentioned it

in a brief paragraph under Globe (pop. 6,419) as
winding "for many miles." But locally it has the
reputation of being second only to the Grand Canyon, and it lives up to its reputation. We stopped
several times and looked, and got out, and peered
over. We said, "Just *look* at that!" and "How
would you describe it?" and "We must remember
this."

The names of places got better, though they
stayed small while the country got bigger and bigger. We drove from Globe to Show Low (com-
memorating a famous poker game), past gradually
opening mountain vistas that passed belief. At Clay
Springs it was cold and there was old snow in
patches on the ground. Hoping for lunch, we
stopped at an inviting log-cabin lodge. No room,
not even for a meal, but the helpful landlord di-
rected us to the White Mountain reservation of the
Apaches, where, he said, there was a quiet and remote motel owned and operated by the Apaches
themselves. Would it be tepees, I wondered, or a
long house? And would we share our quarters with
mangy dogs and fleas?

It turned out to be very much better than that—
in fact, one of the three most pleasantly memorable
stopping places on our trip. The motel was a group
of log cabins, spaced well apart in a pinewoods, the
nearest of them at least two hundred yards from
the road, which in any case was not much traveled.
The cabins were the best we had seen anywhere:
the spacious rooms wainscoted in unpainted wood,

with plenty of closet space, good bathrooms and completely equipped full-size kitchens. The name of this peaceful lodge was Hon-dah, which was Apache for "Be my guest." We gratefully accepted the invitation and stayed four days.

"It's the first really silent place we've found in America," said M.

At Hon-dah, besides the motel cabins, there were only the manager's cottage, a couple of stores and a gas station. We couldn't find the manager for two days; he was over at McNary, a nearby lumbering town, where his wife was in the hospital, having a baby. (She came home four days after the baby was born, and was up and about in six.) An Apache woman in the motel office showed us around and gave us our pick of the cabins, which were all empty.

The oil heater in our cabin was ornery, and an Apache boy came to regulate it. Like all the Apaches we saw, he had an enormous square head and seemed muscle-bound. He squatted on the floor by the heater, puffing and groaning with effort and vexation, and finally gave up. He said, "I don't know what in hell's the matter. Maybe when the manager comes back, he'll know some trick to fix it." This was by far the longest speech we heard from an Apache. Mostly they said "Hello" and no more; they speak English badly and with an accent. The manager's wife told us they were "reluctant to speak it."

The Apaches we saw here and at McNary and

along the road to White River looked like a conquered but not a subject race. They were very dark, and as ragged and poor as gypsies. The men all had big square heads and most of them strong bodies; they wore black hats and blue jeans, the trousers belted below their hipless hips. The women were chunky, in long squaw skirts. The children, who had not yet learned dignity but whose black eyes sparkled with life, were everywhere.

In the general store at Hon-dah a young Apache mother was suckling her baby. From his chamber pot on the floor, a three-year-old shouted at her. Though her eyes were fastened on the blaring TV screen, loud with a galloping, shooting Western, she was talking softly to the impatient child. Perhaps she was telling him to be a man and get on with it.

***

Thunderbird Lodge, Chinle. By now we're so used to the standardized, sterilized amenities of the Western motel that this one, which has more personality than any other we've encountered, depressed us at first sight: drab gray stone cottages as uninviting as Welsh hovels, and each with a different type of gas heater—"foolproof" but requiring the hand of an expert—worn floors, peeling plaster walls, faulty plumbing. But the beds were extremely comfortable, the furniture was charming, the hostess human and hospitable. She invited us to dinner, at six-fifteen: thick vegetable soup, enormous hearts-of-lettuce salad, colossal steaks with corn, mashed potatoes and peas, lemon meringue pie, continuous black coffee (she herself drank eight cups of clear tea).

Besides ourselves and Mrs. B., an elderly couple, natives of Arizona. Nobody asked us any questions. Mrs. B. turned out to be Italian-born. The elderly couple talked about their three foster children— one Korean, two Italian—to whom they had written and sent money for the past seven years.

▀▀▀

In the Petrified Forest and the Painted Desert you get a glimpse of geological time. They tell you that all this goes back 160 million years. That's too far and too fast, from the slow-moving pinpoint of the present, but it does give you a quick sidelong eyeblink. I tried to imagine this land as having "just" (oh, a thousand years or so before) emerged from under the sea. It has a sea-bed look to it, if you can get over the notion that the bottom of the sea is flat—is, in fact, mountain and desert and valleys, broad as a day's journey or deep as a gouged-out canyon.

▀▀▀

An Indian trader in the Southwest was asked if he would sell his business. He said he might, and even agreed to put a price on it: five thousand dollars in gold. But when the prospective buyer brought the cash, the trader said, "I got to have fifty thousand more for the view."

The most beautiful land we saw in the Southwest was in the Indian reservations. It was also the most barren. But in these days when uranium—and what other hidden treasure?—has become a greater prize than gold, the desert may blossom like the Bomb. If the Indian lands turn out to be extremely valuable, or, even more, if they are found to contain sizable deposits of minerals "necessary to the national safety," how long will the Indian owners be left in undisputed possession?

The Hopi, a poor but proud tribe, have set their faces against any such "development"; if there are riches buried under their rocky mesas, they are determined not to disturb them. But their neighbors the Navajos have begun to cash in. In 1959 the Navajo tribal council, from leases, royalties and rentals on oil, helium and natural gas, had an income of about $28 million.

▲▲▲

One reservation M. had heard about and wanted to see was Acoma (accented on the first syllable, a flat *a*), so we went there, and it was worth every bump in the bad road. We curved into a broad valley of sand and sagebrush, lined by ancient mountain walls; on the valley floor stood two mesas, the first as symmetrical as a castle. There were no visible traces of human habitation, but it had been the original site of the Acoma pueblo, which we could see crowning the second mesa.

The road to the top was precipitous, and there was a sign warning visitors not to attempt it in a car, so we clambered up on foot. The adobe town seemed nearly deserted: a few Indians were repairing some of the old houses and building new ones. One attached himself to us as a guide and showed us around the old church and the parochial school, which he said was the first schoolroom in America.

Beyond the low churchyard wall, crenellated by a series of pat-a-cake sculptured (and much weathered) heads, the steep downward slope of the mesa was cluttered by scores of ramshackle privies.

Walking through Acoma's narrow streets, we were hailed by an Indian woman who wanted to sell us souvenirs. We settled for a colored postcard, a crude travesty of this spectacularly beautiful place. The price: twenty-five cents—five times what it should have been.

The woman told us that the Acoma were "a big tribe"—seventeen hundred of them; but there was room for them all in this pueblo. At this season most of the tribe worked on the plains and climbed up to Acoma only for weekends. We wondered how anyone whose birthright included the marvelous sweeping view from that mesa could ever bring himself to forgo it. But perhaps the sight had palled on them; or perhaps, like the equally "fortunate" inhabitants of Italian hill towns, their poverty was stronger than this eye-delighting prospect. We were luckier and could look our fill with no such underthoughts.

But who can describe this country? All you can do is to take a double handful of large colored adjectives and make a messy blot on a piece of paper. Not a good likeness. A straightforward Western, with a wide screen and in Technicolor, does better.

Nevertheless, I was moved to attempt a description of Acoma:

> *Three tin cans in a corner of the cemetery,*
> *Mud walls around it, topped with funny faces;*
> *An old adobe church, smutching there on all*
>   *fours,*
> *And the sides of the mesa tumbling down, the*
>   *privies out of the wind.*
> *Look away, and what do you see? Miles of*
>   *golden air,*
> *Flat surround of tawny desert, monuments of*
>   *rock,*
> *A silent valley, an old dry land,*
> *The limits are table-topped mountains, stony*
>   *and final.*
> *Who did this, that makes you catch your*
>   *breath, and cares nothing?*
> *Look away, look again.*

━━━

The post office in an Indian reservation, at a place called Chambers. A weathered shack, combination general store and post office; nothing else but a few smaller shacks. On the floor, just under the general-delivery window, an Indian asleep (drunk? anyway, asleep).

Standing on a high mesa at Shungopovi, talking to a Hopi chief who looked the part although he was dressed like a poor workman and had the surprising name of Dick McLane. He said he needed a few white turkey tail feathers to wear in the next ceremonial dance. Eagle feathers used to be the thing, but there are no eagles now. I asked him if he knew a friend of mine in London who had often visited the Hopi reservations. He did indeed and asked me for his address; he said he thought his son-in-law owed my friend a dollar.

···

"What *is* there about this Western country, M.? They throw it all away, and yet something—something all-desirable, something amazing—still remains. They roam around it like dogs trying to find a comfortable place to lie down in; they never find it, or, if they do, they bark too much to be convincing. Is it because they were born here?"

"They weren't born here."

"And yet I'm convinced they love it."

"Why?"

"Because, damn it, it's a will o' the wisp, it's the most, it's a new discovery, it's hope."

"You're drunk."

"Yes, I am. But it's a hell of a fine country."

10

All for Your Comfort

In Albuquerque the eyesight of the people we met was so dazzled by the light of the future that they saw nothing incongruous between their graceless, unlovely town and the mountains and deserts of their tremendous countryside. The main street of Albuquerque: perhaps even New Mexicans wouldn't enter it for a beauty prize, but it could stand in for almost any main street in any American town. It reminded me of that old Western yippee, one of those cowboy yells that flare up from a whirl of high spirits, barroom boastfulness and the intoxication with space that all true Westerners feel: "Powder River! A mile wide, an inch deep, and God knows how long!"

Central Avenue, Albuquerque's main street, is not unusually wide, but it does give the impression of being only an inch deep, subject to flash floods and the inundation of the next cloudburst of new construction; and God knows how long it is—it must go petering out and picking up again for a good fifteen miles. Along this nearly dry river bed, waiting for a solid stream to fill the channel, the town trickles along: slapped-together wooden boxes of shabby little stores; bigger, newer boxes of brick and glass and chromium; vacant lots with tattered fences and piles of trash; gas stations on every other corner, streamered with signs and slogans, crowded with secondhand cars for sale; "eateries" and "niteries," hamburger heavens, cocktail lounges, painless dentists, shoeshine parlors, motels, morticians.

It's all there, everything the citizens of Albuquerque want—everything but beauty and convenience, whose absence they haven't noticed. They drive through this long-drawn-out drabness with the impunity of happy blind men. And they all drive; they have to. They think it quite natural that the drugstore, the bakery, the bank, the post office should be so far away that you have to take a bus or a car to get there.

▪▪▪

In Tucson we discovered, by lucky accident, a Spanish writer, Señor R., whom M. and I much admired. He had fought for the republic in Spain's civil war and was now a refugee. We spent an evening at his house, a stucco ordinariness which he had managed to Europeanize partly, by making the garage into a big room with a fireplace and a billiard table, covered with his papers. His wife brought out a bottle of wine, and the conversation was animated though difficult. It was for me, at least, as a gramophone was playing Catalan music, and R., who stood up all the time or strode around the room, talked tumultuously in a mixture of Spanish and heavily accented English. M. understood him, however. She said he was like "a Spanish bull with brains."

When she asked him how he liked the United States he said, "It is like living in limbo; not unpleasant, but limbo." Americans, he said, are "very nice, very good, they have very fine cars. They roll very fast, but there is no hurry. They make love without love, they eat without hunger, drink without thirst. They are innocent; but if they do not in two generations find substantial values there will be bad—dangerous—trouble."

Who is there he can talk to?

"Nobody. You." Anyhow, who talks of life and death here?

He could not go back to Spain, except to kill Franco—"and that's not work for an honest man."

He spends his days writing and painting. The house was filled with his pictures, large, colorful, symbolic—of what? Not of limbo.

▰▰▰

Contents of my bathroom at Western Skies Hotel (a supermotel) at Albuquerque:

Wall container with Kleenex
Electric heater
Wastebasket
Wall brackets over washstand for
  a. ashtray
  b. toothbrushes
  c. "shoe mitten"
4 bath towels
4 face towels
4 washcloths
4 small cakes of soap (wrapped)
2 tumblers, wrapped in wax paper on which
  is printed: "This glass has been sanitized
  and carefully wrapped to keep it clean for
  your personal use."
Band of paper bisecting toilet seat—"Sanitized
  for your protection."
2 envelopes, each containing two aspirin pills;
  envelopes marked:

> Never a Headache
> under the
> WESTERN SKIES
> Aspirins for you—
> Another Western Skies Service
> Ralph Hitz, Jr.,
> General Manager
> An Associated Federal Hotel

Bathmat and rubber mat for shower—"This
  bathtub mat is placed here for your convenience and protection . . . to make your
  stay with us more enjoyable."
Walls and floor completely tiled; ceiling fitted

with perforated anti-noise panels, exhaust duct.

Hitches: only place to put toilet articles is a too-small glass shelf over the water closet; no rail or any place to hang towels; the washbasin is inconveniently small—and so is the whole bathroom; the plastic shelf for soap in the bathtub is too big for its niche and clatters down at the smallest nudge; the toilet-paper roll is set awkwardly far away from the seat.

"For your comfort and convenience." Does this cantrap mean anything at all? Or is it just, as they say, "a form of words"?

＊＊＊

Omi had been trying to read Mencken.

"I don't *like* him," she said. This was violent talk, from her, and I was curious to know what had roused it.

Later, as I was looking through the cast-aside book, I thought I found the passage that had decided her. It was on patriotism.

> Patriotism [wrote Mencken] is conceivable to a civilized man in times of stress and storm, when his country is wobbling and sore beset. His country then appeals to him as any victim of misfortune appeals to him—say, a street-walker pursued by the police. But when it is safe, happy and prosperous it can only excite his loathing. The things that make countries

> safe, happy and prosperous—a secure peace,
> an active trade, political serenity at home—are
> all intrinsically corrupting and disgusting. It
> is as impossible for a civilized man to love his
> country in good times as it would be for him
> to respect a politician.

If Mencken or anybody else had ever tried that
kind of thing in Omi's presence, she would have
said, "Don't talk such nonsense!" As it was, she
simply turned her back on him.

Omi's sharpest comments were invariably un-
spoken—either wrapped up in a kindly fuss of ir-
relevant, embarrassed but determined small talk or
stated in her calm, cheerful but completely with-
drawn presence as she wrote a letter or read a book
or played a hand of patience; much as Duse could
express to an audience, by her silent profile, the
fact that incest had been committed. Though always frustrated, once in a while I tried to lure Omi
into saying something derogatory. No, she wouldn't
even *join* me in it.

In my considered view, the vanilla milk shake,
one of the glories of America, had gone to hell since
my last visit. You still got a whole shakerful—
enough for two glasses, and sometimes a bit more
—but now the concoction was so stiff with ice
cream that you had to mumble and mouth your
way through it like a caterpillar, you couldn't drink

it. Also it was sickly sweet, too much vanilla. Eventually I learned to persuade the soda-jerk: "Go easy on the vanilla. And just half the amount of ice cream you usually put in." But that remedy occurred to me only after long experience; I am not a fast man with a new idea.

Once Omi and I were having a milk shake together.

"Don't you find that a little too sweet, Omi?"

"Well, not for them."

11

Texasity

"How can you call yourself a good American," said M., "when you've never been to Texas?"

"Well, I've met Texans."

M. said that was not enough; people learned only by personal suffering. She had been in Texas several times and wished it to be known, right at the start, that she was now too old and too weak to stand more than two days of the place. Omi felt that M. exaggerated as usual and there was no call for this pessimism, though one had to admit that Texas was a bit too big.

We stayed in Dallas for five days. It was Culture Week. Luckily none of us liked opera; every seat for the week's performances was sold. The musical climax of Culture Week was *Medea*, with Maria

Callas in the title role. The literary highlight was
a book-and-author luncheon, held in the ballroom
of the brand-new Sheraton Hotel, at only five dollars a plate and with three famous authors as guests
of honor. Thanks to an old Dallas friend of mine
named Holland, who was well connected, Omi and
M. and I not only got free tickets but were seated
at the high table, and we had to take a bow when the
toastmaster read out our names.

The toastmaster was the literary editor of one
of the Dallas newspapers. His name was Lon Tinkle;
he was a short, well-knit, swarthy man with a hawk
nose and black mustache, an air of confidence and
a voice like an oboe. He announced that this was the
first book-and-author luncheon that Dallas had ever
had, and that it was a great success: there were 1,003
people present, and this figure exceeded the best
that such cultural centers as Cleveland, Detroit and
Washington, D.C., had been able to show. He introduced our three famous writers: Kay Thompson,
a night-club entertainer who had hit the jackpot
with a series of little books about a terrible child
called Eloise; Moss Hart, the Broadway producer
and playwright, whose autobiography, *Act One*,
was leading the best-seller list; and the Duke of
Bedford, who had also published an autobiography,
but whose principal claim to fame was that he had
turned his ancestral home, Woburn Abbey, into a
profitable tourist center.

All three were lean, attractively nervous, and
winningly or amusingly deprecatory about them-

selves. Kay Thompson confessed that she was not really a writer; so did Moss Hart—adding several funny stories against himself to prove that he was just a lucky fellow; while the Duke of Bedford, who made the biggest hit, went so far as to confess that he hadn't written his book at all, he had simply talked large parts of it to a writer friend.

The audience was warm, appreciative, laughed steadily and applauded often. When Lon Tinkle declared the proceedings at an end, scores surged to the high table to shake hands and get autographs from the visiting great. M. caught my eye and as usual saw what I was thinking.

"I would have," I said. "Like a shot. But nobody asked me."

▀▀▀

I was amazed, as I always am, at the discomfort and inconvenience with which politicians have surrounded the simple act of getting a drink. In Dallas, if you want wine with your dinner, you must first go to a wine shop and buy a bottle, which you then take to the restaurant with you, decently clothed in a paper bag. This is the standard procedure. As for getting a drink in a bar, that's impossible; there are no bars. As usual, the rich and privileged have found ways of getting around the law. My friend Holland took us to the Cipango Club (millionaires only, to judge by the furnishings and the food and drink) and there the bar was running with the smooth fierceness of "21."

I think M. was more impressed by the Texasity of Dallas than I was. At the Cipango Club we met an elderly cattleman with white mustachios and a gaudy waistcoat, who treated us to several drinks and informed us that General George Marshall, the late Secretary of State, had deliberately given China to the Communists and was the biggest traitor this country has ever had. The government itself, of course, is not much better; about the only business it hasn't yet messed up is the cattle business, and if it ever does, by God he was getting out of it.

And when we went to see an oilman I knew, one of the big "independent operators," he told us about a Texas superstition that shocked M. even more. That day, he said, he had picked up four gallons of chile at the Oilmen's Club and brought it home— just in case. When oilmen are hard up, he said, they fall back on eating chile, so he always has some on hand.

One night we went to dinner at a Polish restaurant, the Old Warsaw, where the proprietor was a former cavalry officer; the headwaiter was a Ph.D. from Cracow University. The food was good, and we brought our own wine. M. is an old Poland hand, so the evening got off to a good start. It went on well, too; somehow we fell into a discussion of the Civil War, and our young waiter, who turned out to be a Georgia boy, became so interested that he joined in. According to him, it would have been much better if the South had won; in that case, the

whole country would now have more stability and
better traditions.

▰▰▰

The famous Neiman-Marcus department store
disappointed us, except in the fabulousness of its
prices. Was it the slightly old-fashioned look of the
building, and the conventional arrangement of the
goods for sale? Certainly they were luxurious
enough. I thought I wanted an overcoat and asked
to see one of vicuña; the cheapest Neiman-Marcus
had was one for $450. No sale. All the same, the
salesman said, "It's been a pleasure to know you."

▰▰▰

"I'm beginning to believe," M. said, "that I must
be deeply happy and live in the finest city on earth."
"Why?"
"Because I never talk about it. These Texans are
fishy beyond words. No sane outsider would be
convinced by *anything* they say about Dallas, so
who are they trying to convert? Themselves?"

▰▰▰

The formal farewell in Texas—from new ac-
quaintances, from shopkeepers, from everybody—
is "Come back and see us." In Gulf Coast Florida,
which is deeper South, it's "Y'all come back," or
sometimes "Y'all come back, y'heah?" This is kindly
meant, I'm sure, or at the least a polite convention,
but when you hear it from a hard-faced Florida

cracker, his eyes like deep little belly-buttons sunk in craters of fat, it has a challenging or sinister ring.

At the airport in Tallahassee we picked up our fourth and last "drive-yourself" car, and the fanciest: a carnation-red Chevrolet, with gold-braid trimming around the upholstery. In the hushed mild air we set off along the coastal road, into what M. called "the pea-brained, talkative South."

She and Omi had been along this way some years before, when the coastal country was sparsely settled between its sleepy small towns and weathered-shanty villages. Now they found it greatly changed; the population explosion had reached Florida too. The landscape itself looked explosive. The long sandspit paralleling the coast bristled with radar towers and missile bases; we passed a motel that called itself "Missile View"; Fort Walton's Chamber of Commerce proclaimed it "the town of the Sonic Boom." The old-fashioned hotel Omi and M. remembered from earlier days was still there, but it had changed management and was just beginning to struggle up from its nadir; moreover, the view across the sandspit was now sawtoothed by the pill-boxes and towers of the sonic installations.

The farther we went the more built up the coast appeared. But then, on that barren shore, we made a lucky landfall. The sandspit had run itself under, the scrubby trees had disappeared, there was nothing between the road and the sea but sand and the long blockhouses of motels, when we saw a side road heading for the water, at this point several hundred yards away, and a large sign pointing to a motel on the distant beach. We turned, we drove in, and found at last the peaceful place we had been looking for.

It was one of these self-contained motels with dining room attached (it also turned out to have a night club of sorts on the top floor, but by luck or the dexterity of the architect no sound from it ever disturbed our sleep) and a swimming pool on a terrace facing the sea; otherwise it was like hundreds of others, with one rare and notable exception: it was far enough from the highway. And our rooms looked out over the broad, dazzling white beach to the huge expanse of the Gulf.

We settled in with a sigh of content. Other travelers came every afternoon and left the next morning; we stayed on and on, and spent two happy weeks there.

➤➤➤

The almost-deserted beach, an endless sandspit stretching both ways farther than the eye can reach. Sandpipers fussing busily along the water's edge, congregations of sea gulls, drab-bodied, leathern-winged, rising lazily and flapping away. The dead bird, its body lying careless and heavy where the sea has left it, its head cocked crookedly half under it, and the maggots already at work. The snow-white sand, faintly yellow where the waves have spilled over it, the sea's stain.

➤➤➤

Sitting on my screened-in balcony and squinting out at the dazzling Gulf, I tried to think. We had come almost to the end of our journey; we had covered thousands of miles, by plane, train and car, through large parts of my own country that were new to me. What did I make of all that?

I frowned at the Gulf and stuck out my lower lip, an action I have sometimes found an aid to thought. Not this time, however. The Florida sunshine, the dancing light on the water, the silence, erased my languid efforts and lulled me into a doze.

I was bowling along the Massachusetts Turnpike in a green Volkswagen. We were heading for Boston. But this time "we" were not Omi and M. and I. The companion sitting alongside me (in what he persisted in calling "the death seat") was an oddly shaped fellow named Charles. This was all quite in order. Our expedition over, Omi and M. and I had separated; later, with the uneasy feeling that something still remained to be done, I had written to M. that I was thinking of returning to America for another look. She had sent an encouraging telegram in reply: "Even Columbus had another go. Now you can fill in the chimps."

It never occurred to me that the final word, "chinks," had reached me in garbled form; I immediately began to wonder how to find these "chimps" I was to instruct. Of course: my zoologist brother-in-law, who had considerable influence at the Bronx Zoo. And that was how I came to be driving through Massachusetts with a chimpanzee named Charles. He had been represented to me as most intelligent, and I must say he listened to me at first with what appeared to be rapt attention. As the trip progressed I became less and less sure that he took in anything I said to him. His expression was inscrutable, and he had some very odd habits.

"If you're going to spit," I said to him, "for God's sake put the window down!"

Charles gave me a sliding, sidelong look, at the same time twirling the window handle expertly with one hairy finger. The faintly scratchy hoarse sounds from his throat became a chaotic rumble, as if he were preparing to move out of his body. Oh, for the good old days with Omi and M. on the open road. . . .

I came to with a start, blinking my eyes at the hypnotizing dazzle of the sun-hammered Gulf. This was not getting me anywhere. Think? Too sleepy. I yawned and staggered in to my bed for a much-needed rest.

▲▲▲

Our trip really ended in Florida. From there we went our several ways: Omi back to her beloved garden of St. Louis, which always needs her endless cultivation; M. to Europe, large parts of which annoy or enrage her but in which on the whole she feels at home; and I to New York, because I always go there when I'm anywhere near it.

The Silver Meteor, crack train of the Seaboard Air Line, is standing in the Jacksonville station, waiting to pull out for New York. Only eight minutes to go, and you suddenly remember you want to send a telegram. Too late to risk the long tunnel back to the waiting room; what to do? Ah, there's a uniformed girl attendant, obviously some sort of factotum; she should be able to help you. Yes, in a way. She tells you where to find a telegraph blank: in the observation car—150 yards away, at the back end of the train. Write your telegram, she says, and then bring it to her. And you do; you have to run only the last seventy-five yards. Wouldn't it have been more comfortable and convenient if she had produced a telegraph form from her satchel? It would.

You ask a porter, stationed beside his Pullman on the platform, for your car, number 48. Does he answer, "Right here, sir; this is it"? No, he doesn't. He gives you a withering stare and says disdainfully, "Why, it's right here!"

You want a drink before dinner, so you walk back seven cars to the observation lounge. The car is loud with drunken women, but there is no service, and when you ask the Negro behind the bar for a cocktail he says, "You want the *Pullman* lounge? That's up ahead—ahead of the second diner." When you get to the second diner, the steward wants to show you to a seat, and you say you're just going to have a drink first. He tells you, two cars ahead.

Does he tell you, or does anybody, that when you get there you can't *get* a drink? No, he lets you find that out from the Filipino steward, who informs you that no drink except beer can be served until the train has crossed the Florida-Georgia line, at seven-fifteen (it is now six). As you reel back through the first-class diner, you say bitterly to the noninformative steward, "No drinks in Florida!"

"Oh, no, only beer."

⁂

The surfaces of the streets in New York, both avenues and crosstown, were more than ever like washboards: so ridged, buckled and pitted that passenger cars and taxis bound and leap like kangaroos. But everyone is accustomed to this, so no one seems to notice. Neither does anyone notice, apparently, that at street level the air literally stinks—and you can see as well as smell the cause: the penned-in traffic with its hundreds of thousands of roaring exhausts farting out dark fumes.

But there is one extraordinary change in New York street manners: pedestrians have ceased to be the helpless and wary quarry, fleeing for their lives before the charging traffic, and have in their turn developed an almost brutal disregard for the rights of drivers. It is now a rule, sternly enforced, that a car turning a corner must stop and wait until the stream of walkers halts to let it through. A few years ago, a taxi would have plunged into the crowd, its strangled horn blaring and its driver spitting insults; now I frequently saw two or three taxis waiting at a standstill to turn the corner, often held up so long that the lights would change. The faces of the drivers were something to see, but none of them said anything; they just sat there and took it.

What could have happened to them to reduce them to this pseudo-meek state? At the very least, I imagined, half a dozen of them must have been hanged and left dangling as an example. The survivors certainly gave the impression of men obeying the rule of politeness with a gun at their backs.

On a cross street just off Park Avenue a steely old panhandler approached me, not as a beggar but as one demanding his rights. He put out his hand and said, "I need seven cents to buy a pint of booze." He took my dime as if it was an insult and shuffled off.

Some days later, passing a brownstone front, I was accosted by another old man, huddled on the steps. I paid no attention to his mumble and walked on. Then guilt overcame me; I went back and gave the old man a dollar. That evening, after I'd forgotten all about it, I walked past the same house, and there he was on the steps, sprawling dead drunk in his vomit. Three children stood and watched him with grave interest. If they had known my part in it, I thought, they would have blamed me, and rightly. So much for sentimental charity. Next time, I said to myself, I'll give only what I'm asked for.

▪▪▪

This taxi driver was so hoarse with rage that he seemed in danger of losing his voice. He had just been gypped out of a $2.90 fare. His passenger had told him to drive to a hotel and then had left him to "wait a minute"; he had waited twenty minutes and then gone inside to look; of course the bastard had gone out by another door. I attempted to sympathize. Had it ever happened to him before? Fuel to the flames.

"I been driving twenty-six years, and it's happened to me hundreds of times. *Hundreds of times.* Eight million people out there, and they're all against you. *People hate people.* Never trust nobody, not even if he was your own brother. You know why they do it? Put something over on you. That's what they all want."

I was even more impressed by a taxi driver who said to me, "A man here likes Pennsylvania Dutch egg noodles." Not quite sure that I had heard him correctly, I asked him to repeat this remark, and he did. The only comment I could find was both feeble and rude:

"So what?"

"So nothin'. I just didn't know the Pennsylvania Dutch liked egg noodles."

This left me thinking there was much truth in the saying that to be a New York hackie you first had to have a hole in your head; but a week or so later I noticed the large painted sign he must have seen, advertising Pennsylvania Dutch egg noodles. He'd only been trying to make conversation.

***

(From an article in *Harper's* by its editor, John Fischer): "Millions of New York's residents live in squalor and walk its streets in fear. The city's subways are the most ramshackle in the world, its streets are dirty, both its rivers and its air are polluted, and its police system is ineffectual to control the juvenile gangsters being shot down on school-building steps."

***

(From a full-page advertisement in color in *The New Yorker* of a woman's wrist watch, set in diamonds):

WHAT IS LOVE?

> It is a deep longing for happiness . . . another person's happiness . . . a woman's.
> It is knowing at all times that you can count on his strength . . . and forgive his weaknesses.
> It is a little watch, from him, given with a smile and a kiss. A watch set with flawless diamonds. And one you will wear for life.
> It is two people laughing and laughing . . . for no reason whatsoever.

12

The Huntsmen Are Up

From a plane flying at twenty thousand feet you get a mapmaker's view of the earth. Seen from that height man's world simplifies itself into miniature highways, towns and cities, and large parts of the countryside seem to be uninhabited. From this vantage point our civilization looks neater than it is, but also superficial and patchy. It is even possible to see it as a kind of skin disease on the earth's surface, a precarious yet stubborn growth that spreads here, disappears there and is perhaps not incurable.

Of course, we can't accept the possibility that all the works of man are nothing but a skin eruption, yet we have to admit that civilization and disease have much in common. The record of history, short and uncertain as it is, contains little else but the list of man's savage cruelties to his fellow man and of his greedy attempts to seize everything he thinks worth having on the face of our planet. We are proud of our total achievement, at the same time deprecating the crimes of which it is mainly composed.

Though we have not yet learned to distinguish with any certainty between good and evil, nor how to reconcile our feelings and our acts, we have risen far enough above our animal beginnings to have a bad conscience. Or is it still only an animal fear, a whiff of danger? Some of our forebears thought they had discovered and understood the rules of our world; now we are less sure than ever before that we and those rules may not be at cross-purposes. So we have a new fear, or have reverted to an old one: that as inhabitants of the earth we are not "behaving right"—i.e., as we must behave in order to survive.

We Americans are peculiarly sensitive to this fear. Though our friends have generally kept a tactful silence on the subject and we ourselves don't often mention it, we cannot forget that we were the first human beings who dropped atom bombs on helpless and unsuspecting fellow human beings. It was we who loosed the monster, twice. And so far we have been the only ones. For that act, what will be required of us?

We have other things on our conscience. Some of them are sins committed long ago and almost forgotten that are now coming home to roost. Our treatment of the Indians. Our treatment of the land we took from them. We never regarded the Indians as the rightful owners of America, although they had been living here for some time before we came. We called it God's country and took title to it from Him; the Indians, we said, were too incompetent to be His tenants. We either exterminated them or pushed them away into pockets of barren territory we thought we wouldn't want. We drew up treaties with them, promising them that they and their children would have that land forever. Sometimes we kept those promises; sometimes, when it didn't suit our convenience or our greed, we didn't.

We were in a hurry to take over our new world, and the Indians were only a hindrance. Often the country itself was another. When you see a remnant of forest wilderness like the Olympic National Park you get an inkling of what dogged fury it must have demanded to clear enough ground for even a small farm. The early pioneers were so busy trying to survive that they couldn't be bothered about preserving anything but themselves. It was them against the land, and if their first enemies were the Indians, their second must have been the trees.

The impetus that carried the pioneers across the Great Plains and over the mountains and through the forests necessarily had a destructive cutting edge—clear the land, clear away the Indians, clear a right of way for the roads and railways. Until at last they had opened the country right to the Pacific, the pioneers must have felt hemmed in by huge natural obstacles. And even then, they had been in such a hurry to get there, to stake out their claim to the whole midsection of the continent, that they left a lot of blank spaces behind them.

And just at that point came the bloody interruption of the Civil War, that useless, envenoming, hopeless family quarrel, turning aside the impetus that was driving the pioneers West. When the end of the war released the pent-up drive, its final stages were crueler, uglier, more damaging than otherwise they might have been. The bison and the antelope were exterminated, the last free Indians killed off or rounded up, and the "bad man" became the Western hero.

The pioneers and the early settlers were rugged, ax-wielding men; they chopped down trees and plowed up prairies and shot game as if all these things were inexhaustible. There was more than enough of God's plenty, there was too much of it, in the America of their day. And they were a few harmless amateurs compared to the regiments of professional despoilers who have come after them.

America is a big country, as everyone can see—not quite as big as Brazil, nowhere near as big as Russia or China, but still very large, as nations go—and it's surely not strange that Americans themselves are more aware of this bigness than anybody else. We don't feel cramped or crowded yet (except in gopher holes like New York), our great open spaces still give us an invigorating sense of money in the bank, capital waiting to be used. Not being miserly, but on the contrary notoriously generous or even spendthrift in our ways, we have never made much distinction between spending income and spending capital. Although we are uneasily aware that our natural resources are finite and that we are using them up at an extravagant rate, at the same time we reassure ourselves that this irreplaceable capital is in effect replaceable—there's so much of it still left or we can always find substitutes. Though we can see our riches pouring down various drains, on the whole we simply don't believe that America's cornucopia could ever stop gushing out dividends.

I love thy rocks and rills.

Yes, in bits of New England and in national parks, off season.

I love thy blasted rocks and thy polluted rills,
Thy burned-out woods and pylon-stapled
hills.

***

Our taking over of the best part of the continent may have been more like a rape than a love affair, but it was nothing compared to the way we have "developed" the country since. Along the eastern seaboard the scars of our first beachheads have spread and thickened; the almost continuous welt of our factories and ugly towns girds the coast from Boston to Baltimore. The Atlantic shore could never have been beautiful, but wherever it was worth our while we have made it hideous. Two generations ago South Amboy, now an industrial slum, was a quiet summer resort. Every New York-bound commuter daily endures the poisoned expanses of the Hackensack Meadows, that swampy shantyland where even factories fear to tread; if he no longer winces at the sight—and at the stink of the nearby factories—it's because of his air-conditioned train and his squalor-conditioned eyes.

Driving past Newark on the New Jersey Turnpike, even a blind passenger would know where he was by the horrible smell of cooking chemicals; as he also would if he took a boat down the Kill van Kull, where the acid refuse of the squatting chemical plants stains the water like insect blood. A thousand miles to the south, the dismal beaches of Florida have been reclaimed from cypress knees and Spanish moss for crowded bungalow cities and the clustered towers and artificial islands of Miami Beach, a fabricated paradise that could seem desirable only to the vulgar rich and their envious admirers.

The spacious land that we still have most of, and that most attracts us, is in the West. We gave it the treatment the first time over, but only hurriedly: we plowed up the prairie grass, killed the buffalo and let in the dust; hastily we tore bald patches in the forested hills. But there's a lot left. There are still millions of acres of trees waiting to be cut down, hundreds of half-built towns hoping to puff themselves into littler Los Angeles (which itself has not yet encrusted the whole of southern California); the deserts of Arizona, Nevada and New Mexico have only begun to blossom with beer cans, gas stations, trailer camps and motels. But all this is under way, and with shining eyes it moves. The Russians, with their pathetic five-year plans, seven-year plans! We have a plan for the millennium, starting next year, and already we have marked out the suburbs of the dreadful City of Man.

We have been told but don't yet believe that we have filled our frontiers. We are still "developing" America like the pioneers who went before us, hewing and lopping and jerry-building with no thought of the slow past that gave us our present, and little reckoning of the future beyond the rapid coming of a gilt-edged tomorrow.

The huntsmen are up in America, and their quarry is our country's still-unravaged quietness.

▴▴▴

How does Omi fit into this picture of waste, ugliness, carelessness of the past and disregard for the future? She doesn't fit at all. But she lives in the noisy midst of it; she also must be reckoned a part of the American scene. How do we explain *that?* One of my friends believes that the United States contains a quiet majority of people who are on her side, even if they aren't up to her level; he would say that she is no rarity but a characteristic representative of our country.

I wish he were right; I hope he may be. But the wishful hope reminds me of a line of Georgian poetry that appealed to us in undergraduate days: "O world, be nobler for her sake!" Even at the time, the sentiment had too much sugar in it; it was rhetoric, not a statement of truth. If Omi and her kind are really representative of America, why doesn't the world see and acknowledge it?

The friendly part, the dwindlingly friendly part, of the world does acknowledge it or something like it. Though deprecating our American manners and behavior and our infuriatingly well-meaning, disastrous ignorance, our friends defend us—or think they do, or mean to—by adding that there is something terribly touching, kind and generous about Americans. All very well as far as it goes, but it misses the gist of the best we have; it misses the gist of Omi. How can I explain what it misses?

Once, after a painful conversation with Omi (all she had said might have been broadcast from the housetops, and its gentle generalities wouldn't have made anyone look up), I said to her, "Omi, you're a hard woman!" I meant more than that; I meant, "You're the hardest woman I ever met." America isn't only well-meaning, ignorant, mannerless and infuriating; the best part of it is also hard. It is *capable* of being hard. I mean the word in a good sense: hard against softness, hard against sentimentality, hard against nonsense. Like Omi.

13

These United Wastes

The business of America is business? It might as truly be said that the business of America is waste. Because we make and squander more "consumer goods," by far, than any other nation in the world, we cite this sinister fact with pride as proof that we live—and know how to live, and how to enjoy life —better than any other nation in the world's history. A great many of our products are not useful and are not meant to be used, simply to be torn off or glanced at and thrown away. A great many more are made to be used for only a short time and then scrapped, and we are constantly urged to scrap them long before they are worn out.

Our newspapers are full of bulletins about waste —wastefulness in government spending, the pollution of our air and countryside by "chemical junk," the incalculable social and economic waste that is the net product of the arms race. You might think that these bulletins would be a cause for alarm to an American newspaper reader. If you did, you would be wrong. Either the American newspaper reader didn't read the paragraph (he skips most of the paper most of the time) or if he did read it he discounted it, misunderstood it or didn't take it in. Even if he took it in, he didn't think it would affect *him*. And it never occurred to him, either, that the very paper on which this warning news was printed is in itself a warning. As an American he is so comfortably conditioned to waste that he no longer recognizes a daily sample of it when he holds it in his hand.

Newspapers are made by people like me. But the rough paper on which newspapers are printed is made from trees. Whoever it is that makes a tree, that tree takes a long time to grow big enough to be worth cutting down; and newspapers use up a lot of trees in one year. American newspapers are fatter by far than any other newspapers in the world. Here are the number of pages in a few American newspapers in 1959, for one edition, for one day:

Seattle *Post-Intelligencer* (October 8)	56 pages
Albuquerque *Journal* (November 13)	64 "
Birmingham *Post-Herald* (November 24)	38 "

New York *Times* (December 1)	78	"
New York *Times* (December 9)	92	"
New York *Daily News* (February 22, a Sunday)	716	"

The *News* was proud of this monstrous fatness —which in a human being would be regarded as a dangerous glandular condition—and boasted of it as "this paper's all-time record for size."

The reason U.S. newspapers print so many pages is not because they have so much news to tell but because they run so many advertisements; and that's how they make their money. Does anybody read the ads? The advertisers must think so, for they go on paying. For most Americans, the unwieldy size of their newspapers is a nuisance but hardly noticeable, because they are so accustomed to it. They never think of it in terms of trees, in terms of waste.

We have in America a tradition of waste which in countries less lavishly endowed would long ago have appeared as such a scandalously clear and present danger that it would have been stopped— or cornered by the ruling class as their perquisite. In America, with our enormous margin of safety, waste has been a perquisite common to all but the poorest. Our mystical belief in the virtue of an ever-expanding economy, continually preached by evangelizing advertisers, journalists and businessmen, has become a part of America's patriotic faith in itself, and the hoardings proclaim its triumph even as we smother in tin cans and waste paper. We are so used to waste that we no longer notice it; but we are using up our country to such careless purpose that we are turning it into a gigantic wastebasket, stuffed with the rusting or half-consumed fragments of yesterday's out-of-date purchases. Half the world would make a feast from the contents of our garbage cans, while we tickle our jaded palates with four-color advertisements: what shall we buy next, to eat, drink, wear, ride in or play with?

In man's early days no doubt he hung on to everything that might come in handy, and rarely had two of anything. Now we tell ourselves that we can afford to waste our substance in riotous or gracious living; the days of scarcity are over, and there's always more where that came from. But look who's talking—the Americans. Chinese don't feel that way, or Calabrian peasants, or Poles, or the vast majority of the earth's inhabitants, who haven't enough of anything and have just enough of a few things to keep going, barely. Unlike the rest of the world, we Americans have so many material blessings, superpackaged and gift-wrapped, that we can no longer count them. Nevertheless, we are not so different from other people as we wish we were and try to believe we are: we too share the anxieties of the human condition. And one of the deepest of these anxieties is rooted in our frail and frugal beginnings. Our primitive ancestors must have felt the threatening contrast between their precarious lives and the prodigal, blind power of the world around them. It was only nature, which took a whimsical or murderously indifferent view of man's survival, that could apparently afford to be wasteful.

From the dis-vantage point of human life, nature seemed to be more concerned with experiment—sometimes very rash and extravagant experiment—than with steadiness. In its inhumanly complicated, hit-or-miss methods of reproducing life, in the relentless destructiveness of its floods, droughts, storms and earthquakes, its drownings of islands and continents, its creeping icecaps, its twitchings and shiftings of the whole earth's skin, it showed itself at best neutral, at worst perhaps hostile, to man's frantic effort to establish himself as a permanent resident.

But for a time we thought we had it made and nature licked. Now we don't feel as permanent as we did.

▀▀▀

Since we are accustomed to the American scene, we are largely able to ignore not only the slag heaps, the junk yards and the man-made deserts, both material and mental, that punctuate and underline it, but also the habit of mind that causes and condones this ugliness. Where it becomes depressing enough to attract our attention, we try to explain it away or at least defend it by asserting that it is the inevitable adjunct of progress, of our ever-expanding economy. As a nation we've come to be great believers in what is sometimes called "useful waste." (We still deplore "waste waste" as a kind of slip-up, but we feel that even this sort of squandering may have its experimental uses; anyway, we can afford a certain amount of it.)

Since waste is a sign of progress, it is most glaringly visible in those lucky regions where the population is exploding most loudly—California, the Southwest, Texas and Florida. But all over the United States regional differences are breaking down and disappearing. Even Texans are becoming Americanized. In a few more generations, the only places in the country that may still be noticeably different from the rest may be the stagnant backwaters of New England or the piney barrens of Mississippi and Arkansas.

State boundaries are getting more meaningless every year, except to politicians and lawyers, whose livelihood depends on keeping bailiwicks intact and preserving artificial complications. The United States, which began as an imperfect union, is becoming a unified country. In President Eisenhower's finest hours he used to grope for some statement that was both beautiful and true. He was after something like that when he insisted that he was not so much a Republican President as the President of the whole country. Of course he was; but he meant that he was above faction, and the Republicans clearly didn't like his saying so; they also didn't like his pretty plain implication that he thought it would be a good thing if everybody else felt the same way. The country's united, isn't it? By definition. And now, by gum, we're getting a real togetherness, we're getting unified. We're all good patriotic Americans, so what have we got to disagree about—except, once every four years, who's going to be President of all of us?

And let's dress alike, and think alike, and do everything the Joneses do—if the Joneses are the best we can manage, so far, as neighbors. That way we'll lead a good American life, repeating the fine old slogans about liberty and the hot pursuit of happiness, and keeping in step with the organization ("What's good for the organization is good for the country"). Eisenhower had the right idea about the way things are going, only he couldn't express himself very well. It seemed to him, presumably, a good thing that the United States should "progress" from a union of diverse states (and stubbornly differing individuals) to a unified, increasingly uniform nation of look-alikes and think-alikes.

But that's a German, not an American, idea. Nevertheless, this modern heresy, which would have horrified our forefathers, has taken a deep hold on us.

In politics as in sport, the winner takes all. We don't mind wasting our substance, but we hate "wasting votes." And where does that road lead?

We're the loudest anti-Communist nation in the world. It's funny we haven't noticed that Hitler's Germany and Mussolini's Italy were just as fierce on the same subject—not to mention Franco's Spain and Salazar's Portugal, which still are. When Joe McCarthy was leading his fearless crusade against Communism in the United States, the rest of the world looked on with great interest. It wasn't all those Communists Joe failed to catch that riveted the world's attention, but Joe himself and the unifying effect he had on the shamefaced nation. Old Blood-and-Guts Georgie Patton said that we fought the wrong people in the last war, and there are a lot of Americans, not all of them of German extraction, who still think he was right. Fascism isn't a dirty word in America, like Communism. In fact, it's never mentioned.

When Franklin Roosevelt broke the no-third-term tradition and then smashed it to smithereens by getting elected for a fourth term, he debonairly shouldered an enormous responsibility. On the assumption that he had become the nation's indispensable leader, he so weakened one of the fundamental American rules that in effect he changed it. We have never believed in having a permanent President and would rather let a good one go than run the risk of his turning into a king. We let Washington retire, and shot Lincoln, and have usually preferred mediocrity to brilliance in the White House. One of the great things about America used to be that we didn't hold with great men, or even admit that they had been great, till after they were dead or had gone back to their home towns.

To prevent ourselves from knuckling under to some other Big Daddy, we passed a law forbidding any future President to do what Roosevelt had done. But in letting him have four terms we had succumbed to temptation, and we knew it. If we really want someone to lead us into temptation again, no law is going to stop us.

In union—a union of differences—we found strength. In unity, the closer-and-closer-knit unity toward which we are heading now, we shall find— what? A leader? Yes, perhaps a leader. And perhaps also a "new" nationalistic program like "manifest destiny," with no doubt a national cheer to go with it (remember "Duce! Duce!" and "Sieg Heil!"). A nightmare? Not in these days. Not in a country of sleepwalkers like ours.

▲▲▲

The worst waste in America is the waste of talent. Not so much in the arts, for here socially acceptable abilities are used and rewarded; but more in the huge field of business, where the gifted man is often wrenched, hammered or whittled to size, to fit the uses of the organization; and most of all in public life. As schoolboys we were always being harangued about the duty of the privileged and educated class (ours) to "take an interest in politics"; how else, we were asked, could the country be rescued from the venal and crafty politicians? But we saw what happened to all but the sparse exceptions: either they became venal and crafty politicians themselves or they got nowhere. Like all professions, politics resents and rejects the amateur; and we did not find the professional politician an attractive human being.

Nevertheless, everyone does take an interest in politics, and it seemed and still seems a shameful wrong that under our political system the best men are often excluded or thrown away. Perhaps a great many of us would like to be President of the United States—although I can hardly believe such a thing—but how many of us would scheme and work single-mindedly, month after month, to get the job? Not many, I would say, and not necessarily the best applicants. Yet in the last election the voters had to choose between two men both of whom had been working hard for two years to get the nomination.

In one breath we inveigh against the paucity of talent, the low standards of intellect and integrity, among the men who manipulate the political scene in America, and in the next we condemn as egg-heads, starry-eyed dreamers or has-beens the ablest, most accomplished and most dedicated among us. We are wasteful of our most experienced states-men. By our inflexibly prodigal custom, after they have served one or two terms in the White House or the Cabinet, we have no more practical use for the men who have been the chief executives of our government than to put them out to pasture as respected gossips. They order these things better in Britain. Even in France.

　　　•••

What is it we want? Do we want more and more stuff to buy, and more and more money so that we can buy it, until every family in the United States has at least two cars, two TV sets, an electronic kitchen, college degrees for every member, and a family psychiatrist? Do we want our towns to grow like Albuquerque or Phoenix, our cities like Los Angeles? Do we want to preserve only samples of our countryside in the showcases of our national parks, and let the rest be laid waste by business "enterprise" and real-estate "development"? Do we want the streets of our small towns, the speech and thought and aims of our children, to be interchangeably alike, a pattern of dreary uniformity? Do we want America to compete with Russia in a contest to become the most mediocrity-ridden and ugliest civilization in the world?

Russia and China are bigger than we are, and so eaten by envy of what we have (not of what we are) that they may some day equal and surpass our material prosperity. Until they do, we can justly claim to be the greatest wasteland on earth.

14

How's That Again?

SIWASH UNIVERSITY
CLASS OF 1922
Class Agent
    Hunt Hunter
    1462 Eucalyptus Street
    Pittsburgh 3, Pa.
November 12

DEAR TOM:

I've just returned from Siwash, where our Class Secretary, Joe Brady, and I discussed our Annual Giving, and I'd like to mention a few of the things we talked about.

Last year, 1922 did the best job dollarwise of any class in Annual Giving history. It took a lot of spirit on the part of a great many fellows to do it —and in some cases we know definitely that the contributions represented a real effort. The total, however, was largely due to *exceptionally* generous contributions from four or five men.

We cannot expect these gifts to be repeated—in fact, they were made with the proviso that the major part of each was to be considered as an extra effort.

That means we'll have a lot to make up just to stay even. One of the best ways to do it is to have more men on the team and pushing with us. You've helped us in the past and it would be good to have you with us again. Seventy-five per cent of our Class were contributors last year.

What we're looking for, and hoping for, is not a contribution that will prove burdensome but simply what *you yourself* feel you can afford this year.

In the final analysis, it all boils down to a matter of conscience. If we're really going to show what we as a Class are really capable of doing to help maintain Siwash, we've got to get more fellows into the game.

I hope you'll take a minute to think the matter through. Believe me, we need your help and we'll be more than happy to let you be the judge of what you can do.

Sincerely,

HUNT

November 15

DEAR MR. HUNTER:

Your mimeographed letter, dated November 12, addresses me by my first name, although I have not the slightest memory of ever having met you. And I must add that, if the letter itself is a fair sample of your style, I feel small inclination to make your acquaintance.

Furthermore, I find your request offensive. I take it (though this is not at all clear from your letter) that you wish me to give some money to the university. Your main concern, however, would seem to be the record of the class of 1922 in competition with other classes—"percentagewise and dollarwise," as you would say. Even if I gave a damn about the record of the class of 1922—which I don't—your sales letter would be enough to change my mind. If I should decide to give anything, I shall send it directly to the university treasurer, asking him either not to credit the gift to any particular class or to assign it to the class with the lowest total of contributions.

Faithfully yours,

T. S. MATTHEWS

I didn't send that letter, however; after reading it over I decided that it was too—well, cool. My second attempt was warmer:

DEAR OLD HUNT:

Gee, it was good to hear from you! How are you, old sock? You just don't know how delighted I was to get that old personalized letter with the real old Hunt Hunter touch. You sure have what it takes, writingwise, old man. I can well understand why you are such a notable success in the business world of Pittsburgh, Pa. And believe you me, Siwash is lucky to have you, along with those four other 22ers, on the board of trustees. My, my, I'll bet those other classes wish they had such a fine record.

To tell you the truth, Hunt, I've been feeling kind of guilty lately about not crashing through with my small check to swell old 1922's total. Percentagewise, I guess we stand pretty well, but dollarwise we can always do better, can't we? That's about what I was feeling, kind of dimly, and then along comes your letter and just says it all for me. Boy, when it comes to persuading, you sure can sling that language, Hunt!

Do you know what really got me? I'll tell you. It was where you said that what you're looking for is simply what *I myself* feel I can afford—and one other place, where you say you'll be more than happy to let me be the judge of what I can do. Gosh, Hunt, those are warming words. What I mean is, they made me feel I just couldn't let down the good old class of 1922, that it was up to me to join the team and push with you. I know you've got to get more fellows into the game, and I've been on the bench too long. Hunt, old boy, I'm with you. Here's my check for fifty cents.

Sincerely,

Tom

▬▬▬

The class of 1922 and I spent four years at Siwash, getting educated. Most of us were given a diploma to prove it. Some of us, especially the ones who went on into the law or banking, achieved a command of legal phraseology or business prose; the rest of us had to make out with the grammar our mothers, or somebody, had taught us.

At Siwash the majority of upper-classmen were elected to clubs, of which there were a great many, carefully graded in a social pecking order. Mine, called The Basement, was somewhere near the bottom. But in the thirty-odd years since I was at the university, great changes have taken place there. So everybody says. None of us, for instance, could possibly have passed the entrance examinations nowadays or, if we had squeaked in, could have lasted the course. Everyone has to work much harder now, and there is a new air of Cromwellian earnestness about the whole place.

A reminder of this stern fact reached me the other day, in the form of a large and handsomely mimeographed pamphlet of fifty-three pages, sent to me by my old club. On the cover was printed:

THE BASEMENT PROPOSALS

Some Suggestions for Further Study to Strengthen the Community of Interest between the Undergraduate Clubs and Siwash University

This was obviously no undergraduate production; sure enough, it proved to be the work of the club's board of governors, and the mighty hand of Harvard Law School must have guided its corporate pen. I read the whole thing "with reverence and with awe," in the words of the Siwash hymn. Here is the key passage:

Objectives of the Basement Club Proposals as currently visualized are as follows:

A. To introduce a kind of creative dynamics into the Club enterprise system in the expectation that the Clubs' policies and practices will tend to enhance rather than detract from the University's public position.

B. To do so experimentally at first, so that progress by stages will maximize the demonstration of the procedures involved, and minimize the risk.

C. To end the isolation of the Clubs from those principal outside contacts that could be of constructive help to it—business and the professions on the one hand and the University faculty on the other—and to cement

those ties in support of the University's educational and character-building objectives,
and in a way that will secure undergraduate
support.

D. To develop ways and means of foster-
ing the maturity factor in undergraduate education, as a major objective of the Clubs' op-
erations.

E. To develop ways of increasing the use
of the Clubs' facilities that will at the same
time exert much-needed controls over increasing club costs.

F. To develop ways and means of financ-
ing that will stimulate new contributory
sources and not conflict significantly with
established fund-raising programs of the University.

▄▄▄

Some snobs have said that West Point doesn't
sell as smoothly packaged an education as Siwash
does. But I think there is actually very little to
choose between them. It is true that West Point's
most famous living graduate, President Eisenhower,
used to sound pretty mixed up at times, when he
was answering questions at a press conference or
talking off the cuff; but that was partly due to his
fast-blurting, gobbling manner of speech. And,
after all, you could usually make out, more or less,
what he was trying to get at—which is as much as
can be said about most educated Americans.

The following quotations from Eisenhower are

all taken from the stenographic records of his press
conferences, as reported in the press:

> [*Answering a question about special prob-
> lems in the Farm Belt*]
>
> My program along this line has been re-
> stated time and again. I follow principle, and
> if that is what they want, that is what I will
> give. Otherwise, of course, the American elec-
> torate has its own way of settling the issue.

> [*Commenting on the statement of a disk
> jockey that "payola" was part of the Ameri-
> can way of life*]
>
> The use of air waves, under license from
> the government, for personal gain over and
> above the purposes for which disk jockeys
> are hired is against public morality. And I
> think this fellow, whoever he was, talking
> that way, just had not thought through the
> implications of his alibi.

> [*To a question about whether or not the
> White House press secretary was only the
> President's spokesman*]
>
> Well, he is not—I don't think he is exclu-
> sively either one, because he is certainly not
> my sole spokesman; and he is also an intelli-
> gent, capable staff officer who cannot be ex-
> pected to be—on every question to come in
> and ask me verbatim what my answer is to
> every question, and carry it out to the press.
> Now, for my part, he has done his job well.

And I say in this one, you just go back to him
and talk to him about it.

See? Ike spoke fancy American, but his simple
intention usually blundered through: "I mean well.
I am not a bad man." And that was very reassuring
and made everybody like him and feel that the
country was in good hands. Mamie (as the public
persisted in calling Mrs. Eisenhower), talked simple, straightforward American, and that too was
reassuring. One Thanksgiving Day, when she went
to church but the President didn't, she explained to
the pastor that the Chief Executive was "working
real hard today and couldn't make it."

Simple American speech was characteristic of all
the upper ranks of the Eisenhower Administration
—with the glaring exception of John Foster Dulles,
a Siwash graduate; his massive retaliatory phrases
and agonizing reappraisals sometimes went to the
very brink of international rhetoric. James Hagerty, the greatest White House press secretary
since Roger W. Tubby, always talked good American. When he was asked for a statement about a
passage in Lord Alanbrooke's memoirs (implying
that at a crucial moment in the war Eisenhower had
gone off to play golf when he should have been at
his headquarters), Hagerty said contemptuously,
"I don't even have a no-comment."

And Nixon, though he could ring all the required
changes on political polysyllables when he wanted

to, saw to it that his own family stuck to the good old traditional forms of plain speech. After one of his television appearances in the 1956 campaign, one of his two small daughters welcomed him home with a cry of "Daddy, you did great!"

Some of the purest and simplest American appears in the New York *Daily News,* especially in its headlines:

BOY SORRY

HE SHOT MOTHER

On solemn occasions, such as a big businessman making an important announcement, the American language is capable of an almost Mandarin-like dignity. When the management of General Electric was convicted of rigging prices, one of the top executives explained his resignation in these memorable words: "The relentless publicity involved has severely limited my efficiency."

▲▲▲

Although "good English" is un-American and is, quite properly, regarded by most good Americans with suspicion tinged with contempt (look where it got Adlai Stevenson), we have developed several different *written* dialects that are as abstruse if not so complicated as Mandarin. You can see simple examples on traffic signs in the West, such as "PED XING" (for "Pedestrian Crossing"). In the East, highway signs tend to fancier American ("CROSSING MEDIAN DIVIDER PROHIBITED")—fancy, sometimes, to an ambiguous degree ("RUBBISH DISPOSAL PROHIBITED BY LAW"); but even the scrambled meaning generally gets through ("GO CHILDREN SLOW"). One of these dialects, the artificial lingo in which newspapers are generally written, is sometimes called journalese. It is a somewhat simplified form of the pompous jargon known as "business English"; but it is equally stilted and wordy, and bears little relation to any spoken dialect. Even semiliterate Americans, however, can read journalese and get its general drift. The purest form of this artificial language is found in the New York *Times*.

American journalists learn how to write from reading other American journalists. What's wrong with this system? Nothing much, if only the tomcats set a good example to the copycats. But they don't—they're always getting their paws in their mouths or choking on fishbones too big for them to handle. Although they don't seem to know or care, American journalists nowadays, with a very few glittering exceptions, write damn badly. And their bad writing sets the newspaper style; their low standard fixes the level and shapes the future of the American language.

Just look at this little list. Every word and phrase in it is good American newspaper usage—i.e., good American—and will soon be what we used to call "standard English." I culled these flowers of speech

from one best-selling book. The American journalist who wrote it is a distinguished, competent
professional and all that jazz.

> enormity (he meant "enormousness")
> presently (he meant "now")
> jejune (he meant "juvenile")
> meet with (he meant "meet")
> face up to (he meant "face")
> do you have? (he meant "have you?")
> adverse (he meant "averse")
> hit the beach (he meant "land on the beach")
> beseeched (he meant "besought")
> hail (he meant "hale")
> singlehandedly (he meant "singlehanded")
> jibe (he meant "gibe")

So what? So nothing. The American language is
developing like crazy, as you can see by these by-
blows and thousands more; and the little bastards
breed like ever-loving flies.

▄▄▄

The editorial writers in newspapers—perhaps because they know that almost nobody will read what
they write and that therefore they might as well
talk to themselves—tend to write more colloquially
than their colleagues in the news columns. (The
New York *Times*, which has several editorial writers, who all read each other's editorials, is of course
an exception.) This paragraph is from an editorial
in the Albuquerque *Journal*:

In the field of missiles and other defense weapons, the secretary puts the U.S. in a strong position. The American people want the bad news but they also are deserving of getting the good news. There's often too much smearing and partisan politics by the publicity-seeking and ambitious lawmakers that paints the picture of despair.

This example of good American might have been uttered by President Eisenhower himself.

Editorials are the vermiform appendix of newspapers, a traditional but ineffective relic; the real "movers and shakers" (a favorite American phrase) of public opinion are the columnists. Since they are widely read, or anyhow widely printed—their syndicated columns are the nearest thing America has to a national press—these columnists not only exemplify the American language but have considerable influence on its development. Very few of them write "good English," but they all write good American.

Here's a middle-of-the-road sample, by a columnist named Constantine Brown:

It is difficult for the crystal ball gazers to see what the future holds. But there are indications, derived from reading and analyzing the writings and speeches of the White House apostles who thoroughly prepare Kennedy's thinking, that the overall tendency might lead to domestic welfarism and One-World government paced initially by co-existence with international communism. These are justifiable assumptions since they are based on utterances of Kennedy's professors before they assumed actual responsibilities.

The most specialized and difficult of these dialects are found in the rapidly enlarging field of social studies. Here is a passage from a U.S. Government survey made in a rural community of upstate New York:

> Data support conclusion that each sex regards their same sex classmates as being better able to satisfy their succorance and playmirth needs, at all grade levels. Trend analyses support conclusion of a decrease in mean ratings with increasing grade placement. Mean ratings were generally higher for need playmirth than need succorance. Trends for intra-individual variability indices were in the direction of decreasing variability with increasing grade placement.

▴▴▴

Professor J. Douglas Bush of Harvard was recently quoted in the press as saying that most college freshmen cannot write a page of good English, and that many of them are still only semiliterate when they take their Bachelor of Arts degree. The good American answer to that is "Oh, yeah?"

Language grows; language also deteriorates. Is

there a difference between growth and deterioration? It would be hard to put your finger on it. Perhaps the two are so intertwined that they can't be separated. It's not scholarship that feeds the life-blood of language, but slang, the market place and the sports arena; and which are the arteries, bringing fresh oxygen, and which are the veins, carrying off the used-up blood, it would be beyond human ingenuity to distinguish. Nevertheless, it does seem to some people, including me, that the American language at present is ailing. High blood pressure? By the symptoms, you could also diagnose it as a comatose condition.

The English tongue we brought with us across the Atlantic was an approximate, shifting and lyrical language. The offshoots from Latin, notably French, were obviously more classically exact, and the highest aim of both spoken and written French is still "correctness." Outside such backwaters of pedantry as newspaper offices and schoolrooms, our aim has been for "good English" rather than "correct English." Our tendency (except for the lawyers, who have a language of their own) has been toward loose definitions and a democratic free-and-easiness of expression.

Mencken was not the only one, although I think he was the first, to claim that the "American language" was now the dominant partner in our transatlantic tongue, and that "English" was dwindling into a subsidiary dialect. This view has had some support in England itself. Thirty-five years ago an

Oxford don, George Gordon, saw a striking similarity between the adventurous inventiveness of the Elizabethans and that of the twentieth-century Americans, and deprecated the fixity of "standard English"—and even the static quality of English slang. That was in the Twenties, however, before the last war shook the British out of their established Victorian forms of speech. And the Twenties were a livelier age in America than we have seen since. Now it is we, instead of the British, who are in danger of slowing down into a national conformity.

Our American standards of speaking and writing are not set by people who speak in upper-class accents or who write clearly and well; lest we be thought eggheaded or snooty or otherwise peculiar, we declare our hundred-per-cent Americanism by talking and writing in the same vocabulary, the same vulgarisms, the same tone of voice as "everybody else"—which is to say, in accordance with the semiliterate least common denominator.

Shortly after New York's Mayor Wagner had proclaimed a "Learn English Week," the city started a campaign to persuade pedestrians to obey the traffic rules. The streets were plastered with posters showing a cat named Tweets glaring persuasively; the legend read: "That light's gonna change!" Several people wrote to the papers, calling attention to Tweets' tough talk and asking what effect it would have on children learning English. The mayor's office replied that the object was to shock pedestrians (and thus save their lives), and the kids would just have to overlook the way Tweets talked. Even the New York *Times* had some fun with the story. It pointed out that an earlier poster of Tweets had also "upset the language purists" by saying, "I've got nine lives. Do you?"

Only "purists" could have understood what the *Times* was talking about. In saying "do you (have)?" for "have you?" Tweets was using a perfectly good, universally accepted American phrase. It's not good English, but it's good American; and if Mencken was right, it will soon be good English too. Usage is all; purists and grammarians can only turn their backs to the wind—and later try to pick up the pieces of deadwood. The wind bloweth where it listeth, and there's nothing anyone can do about it.

The only trouble is, that's a little too easy. The people who get blown along by usage say nature is grand, and sure, maybe everybody can't *write* like, you know, those big shots useta, but hell, any kluck can say what he means. You know? Like if he really wants to.

How's that again?

15

O My America!

I have asked myself often whether I am a good American. Perhaps I was asking the wrong person. Or perhaps it is a foolish question. One of the best Americans I ever knew, who served our country more devotedly than most, is already almost forgotten, although when his name is mentioned it is always remembered that he shot himself. Do good Americans ever shoot themselves?

Such a question leads to other questions. Must you be a convert in order to be a true believer? I think many converts incline to think so—or at any rate would say that real faith requires a change of heart, tantamount to conversion. It may be so; but in that case what shall we say of people like me who are Americans neither by their own choice nor by that kind of rebirth which (politicians tell us) produces the dedicated politician? Is it possible to be a good American simply by taking America for granted, as the country in which we were born and which is therefore inescapably and ineradicably ours?

If you were free to elect citizenship in any country in the world, which would you choose? For me, Britain, France, Switzerland, Denmark, Australia all have their attractions, real or imagined; yet I cannot ask myself such a question seriously, only in the spirit of a parlor game. I am an American, whether good, bad or indifferent, and cannot conceive of being anything else. But you couldn't very well call me a hundred-per-cent American. There are many things about my country which I find objectionable or even hateful.

According to our present habit of thinking, any American who criticizes the United States *must* be either a Communist or a Communist tool. By the rules of this silly game, every American has to "stand up and be counted" whenever called upon or whenever he feels called upon. He must reaffirm his loyalty on numerous occasions: when he receives the "privilege" of a passport or takes a government job or happens to be a member of a university faculty thought to contain "subversive elements" or is summoned before a Congressional committee. So at this point I should announce in ringing tones that I am not now, nor ever have been, a member of the Communist Party, that I pledge my allegiance to the flag and swear to up-

hold the Constitution of the United States, so help
me God. Thus I shall "prove" that I am not a disloyal citizen but a good American who loves his
country.

This seems to me not only nonsense but despica-
bly un-American behavior. Nevertheless, it has become traditional practice, and in my lifetime. If
America continues to develop such traditions, then
I hope that my grandsons will refuse to be "good
Americans"—though by that time the penalty for
refusal to conform might be jail or deportation.
Even now all Americans are liable to investigation
by the F.B.I., and their dossiers, a hodgepodge of
facts, allegations and hearsay which they themselves are never allowed to see, are filed in Washington for the "information" of bureaucrats and
Congressmen who might be interested.

I am sure there is a dossier in Washington with
my name on it, for I was once offered a government job and was told that I had been "cleared."
And I must have added, unwittingly, to other people's dossiers. When I had an executive job in journalism I was visited half a dozen times by the F.B.I.
and asked to "tell what I knew" about various
former employees. The agent was always in plain
clothes, always produced his identification card
and always ended his inquiry by asking whether, in
my opinion, the person in question was a loyal
American. I finally got so fed up with this ridicu-
lous probing that I evolved a stock answer: "Well,
I never heard him whistling 'The Star-Spangled

Banner,' but we discourage whistling in this office."

The United States was intended to be a nation of individuals, or at any rate a nation in which everyone could aspire to become or remain an individual. A minority of Americans, I am convinced, still believes that the United States will eventually succeed in being that sort of nation; but only starry-eyed reactionaries will deny that our present development is all the other way. Such a conservative observer as Brooks Atkinson of the New York *Times* has come to the conclusion that "to believe in the original principles of America is to be a dissenter." Except for the bosses—of big corporations, big labor unions and big political machines—fewer and fewer Americans can afford to entertain their egos or dare to invite their souls. Even in their spare time. They can't afford it, and it isn't safe.

Safety first is the present American motto. "National security" is the public, or Pentagon, version; "Be smart" (meaning "Keep in step") is the private translation. And what led us into this rat's alley? Fear. Fear of losing what we've got. Getting what we've got has not made us contented and happy, it has made us discontented and miserable, but the fear of losing it makes us more miserable still. Our forefathers would have been amazed, and ashamed of us. In the present Supreme Court, it is more often than not the dissenting opinions that remind us how we are being hedged in by increasingly protective tariffs on liberty. In a recent dissent Mr. Justice Black said, "This country was not built by men who were afraid and cannot be preserved by such men."

The most un-American activity in the United States is the Un-American Activities Committee. The purpose of this committee is to search out bad Americans, foreign spies, "dangerous and subversive elements" within the country. In practice, this official watchdog of public safety has had as little to do with preserving the republic as the gaggle of Capitoline geese that failed to save Rome. It has been, however, ludicrously and damagingly effective abroad; foreigners regard it as the personification of our national phobia. Have these un-Americans exposed any disloyal citizens, or any evidence of a Communist conspiracy, gnawing away at the foundations of the state? There are spies in every country, and the F.B.I., the secular arm of this Inquisition, has caught a few. But the aroma of roast pig has been snuffed out by the stink of burned-down houses.

One of the basic tenets of English common law, on which our American system of justice is founded, is that a man is presumed to be innocent until he is proved guilty; by the same token, it has been thought better that several guilty men should go free than that one innocent man be wrongfully convicted. The un-Americans, following the practice of the Communists and other totalitarians, deny this civilized axiom and operate on the barbarous principle that it is better to damage the reputation of several innocent people—often, in addition, depriving them of their right to a passport, sending them to jail for "contempt of Congress" (i.e., refusing to implicate other presumably innocent people) or blacklisting them out of their jobs—than to let one possibly guilty person go free. In the cowardly old days of Joe McCarthy, which preceded the dawn of Barry Goldwater and the John Birch Society, the un-Americans invented a useful new category of guilt "by association." They went too far. For now, in the eyes of the world, the United States stands condemned of guilt by association with the un-Americans.

If these bastard Americans are in truth good citizens, then I prefer to be considered a bad one. And I suggest that the un-American Activities Committee should be dishonorably discharged and its annual appropriation handed over to the Civil Liberties Union.

▾▾▾

Americans are sometimes accused of apathy—apathy about the state of the world, about foreign lands (except as tourists), about books, about ideas, about politics (except in the quadrennial popularity contest to decide whether Herman or Verman gets elected President). This alleged apathy is a vexation to all those people who have a specialized or professional interest in these subjects. But in fact most Americans live such crowded lives, what with their jobs, commuting to their jobs, homework, exhausting weekends, golf, television, shopping and spectator sports, that their overloaded days leave them with no time or energy for anything else.

▄▄▄

Is America security-conscious? If that question means anything, I suppose it might mean, do Americans feel insecure? A foreign visitor, seeing the bomb-shelter signs in cities, the notices along highways that "in the event of enemy action this road may be closed to all traffic," the hortatory billboards ("Sleep well tonight—your National Guard is awake"), might be led to the conclusion that Americans are much more jittery than in fact they are. For these scarehead signs and notices are virtually invisible to the American eye; they have been around so long that nobody pays attention to them any more, and if you point one out to somebody he will probably give a small embarrassed laugh and say, "Oh, well."

On the level of world events, I don't think Americans feel insecure enough. More than most people in the Western world they cling to the notion that "it can't happen here, it can't happen to us." (They simply refuse to believe that if it happens to anybody it will most certainly and primarily happen to them. And they refuse to believe that it will happen *altogether*. The incredible depth of their hopeful incredulity is shown by the recent

American craze for investing in "personalized" bomb shelters.) The syncopated screaming of journalism's steam calliopes has become a habitual form of mild entertainment; the cries of "Wolf! Wolf! " from pessimistic pundits fall generally on deafened ears. As the bogey of a fanatically doctrinaire, fanatically intransigent China looms larger on the still distant horizon, the bogey of a perhaps not quite so fanatically doctrinaire, not quite so fanatically intransigent Russia seems to dwindle. Will Russia and China fall out, maybe even come to blows, thus giving the rest of us a breathing space? Might Russia some day need and want our support against a China-dominated Asia?

Since America's leaders obviously have no clear idea of how the future is shaping, nor of how to arrest or control the increasingly threatening drift of events, it is not to be expected that Americans in general should feel much hope beyond an unreasoning belief in their own survival. And yet they do feel hope. To back their belief that "they are the people" they have a long record of luck and success; they are fat with blessings, a very present help in this time of trouble.

Moreover, Americans still believe, or want to believe, in solutions, in finding the answer to any and all questions. The basic reason for our feeling of insecurity is the perception, now spreading slowly but widely among us, that this childish and impatient demand is nonsense. Either the questions that require our answer today are too difficult for us (and *that* we won't yet admit) or we don't understand them.

We are uneasily aware that the atom bombs dropped on Hiroshima and Nagasaki were somehow not quite the right answer to the question of how to win the war against Japan. We are still writhing with uncertainty about our limited answer to the Korean War. And when we went to the polls in 1960 to choose our next President, the man we wanted to show us the way through our maze of thorny questions, the decision was spectacularly indecisive; as the British say, with punning ambiguity, "There was nothing in it."

···

Americans can grow old without growing up. This seems to me a fairer way of putting it than Oscar Wilde did: that America has gone from barbarism to decadence without passing through civilization. Like most Americans, I've been young most of my life (which is far too long to be young), and when we're young we take it for granted that the grownups know what they're doing, even when it's obvious to us that they're doing very badly. And we can see that they run the world, if anybody does; anyway, we certainly don't run it. But now, whether or not I am grown up, I'm definitely middle-aged, and I no longer believe that anybody runs the world except various versions of the Wizard of Oz—or ever has, as far

back as we can see. Perhaps Hadrian, and the An-
tonines. But that was only "the known world," a
small part of the whole, though it gave the illusion
of being all that mattered.

A younger generation than mine has now taken
over the government of the United States, and at
this early moment many Americans, perhaps most,
are feeling hopeful that we may be more quietly
and decently governed. The situation, however, remains the same; our world is a clashing kaleidoscope of jagged particles, in which America is not
the biggest, and it may be beyond the power of
American hands to keep the kaleidoscope steady.

In earlier days I think there must have been a
quality of uniqueness in being an American, but to
a large extent the brightness of that quality has
faded. All nations feel themselves unique; we felt
ourselves more unique than others, and prided ourselves on the feeling, though we must have known
that we owed our fortunate position at least partly
to good luck (we called it Providence). We have
far more of "the good things" of this world than
anybody else has, but apart from these anxious pos-
sessions it would be hard to prove our essential difference from many other nations, or our superior-
ity to them. Nevertheless, Americans still feel like
Americans; and we find it difficult to believe that
other people can love their countries as we love
ours.

Poles love Poland—only God and the Poles
know why. I suppose even Patagonians might feel

homesick for Patagonia, if for some reason they were transported to Montevideo or Metuchen. And Americans in their way love America. I think their way is somewhat different from the European; it must have something in common with people who live in more spacious countries: the Russians, the Chinese, the Australians. It is a particular feeling for the region in which they were born, a general feeling for the whole country. The first is apt to be much stronger than the second; I know Westerners who hate the East and would never willingly go there, Bostonians who despise New York as if it were a foreign city, and Northerners (myself included) who have an unreasoning antipathy for the Deep South.

And when we say "Americans," what do we mean? What indeed. We are an imperfect mixture of immigrants; the only common national factor among us is that almost none of us can properly claim to be an indigenous native or even descended from one. The nearest most of us come to that claim is to say, as Will Rogers is supposed to have replied to a dowager who boasted that her ancestors had come over on the *Mayflower*, "Mine met the boat." Not only do Americans come from different national backgrounds, but some are much more recent arrivals than others. How can a second-generation Czech who has settled in Beacon, New York, be expected to look at the Hudson River Valley with the same eyes as the fifteenth-generation descendant of Dutch patroons? And which one sees it more nearly as it is?

"All men," we were taught to believe, "are created equal"; but somehow we have never applied that dogma to the facts of American life, in which we still have first-class, second-class and even third-class citizens. Suppose we were third-class citizens —poor Negroes or Puerto Ricans (are there any rich Puerto Ricans?); our love for the United States must surely be of a different order from the love felt by our fellow "good Americans."

The question of what it means to be an American gave Henry James more grist than he could grind in his slow, meticulous literary mill; yet he was concerned only with Americans of the very first class. Though they didn't all seem so to him, they must to us, who have so many more classes to choose from. The record of our history is slightly longer than it was in Henry James's day, and it is easier for us to see—or should we say "harder for us to deny"?—that being an American has meant many and contradictory things. The roster of our famous names is a list of quarrels. Some of these men we shot, some we should have liked to hang, some we vilified, some we despised, some despised us. All of them, whether we like it or not, whether we admired them or not, were Americans and are remembered as Americans.

The one thing we can be sure that all Americans agree on is a belief in the future. The future is to be

better than the past or the present, and the future
will be strongly influenced by us. This is part of
the faith of all Americans. But in our picture of the
future we differ among ourselves, not to mention
the rest of the world.

Will history agree with Henry Luce and call
this "the American Century"? Or with Henry
Wallace, who said it would be "the Century of the
Common Man"? Or with Nikita Khrushchev, who
is equally sure that it will be "the Century of Communism"? The Communists also believe in the future, and it is a fundamental of their faith that the
future belongs to them. Perhaps the future will
have to be big enough for everybody, large enough
to contain the multitudes it must.

For the first thing we have to believe about the
future is that the world can survive with double its
present population. Can it continue to live, as we
are trying to learn to do, with the constant possibility of world suicide? Or under the equally immi-
nent possibility of world dictatorship? Can the
Russians, the Chinese, the Indians, ourselves and all
the other peoples of the earth live together in a
world twice or three times as crowded as it is now,
without tyranny and without war?

Unless this future exists, a future in which not
only Americans but all human beings can breathe
and also hope, what is there to believe in?

In this crowded, threatening future, America can
play its part only by being an example to the rest

of the world. Not by preaching or teaching, by charity or by well-meaning missionary ventures. We set an example now, but not one that all the world likes or admires or wishes to follow. Only by becoming in truth the free and civilized nation we claim to be and would like to be can we do our part in shaping the future.

"The American way of life" has become, outside America, either a joke or a threat. That is because the way we live in America is widely misunderstood as being the way we want to live and think we should live—as if we thought America was a finished statement instead of what we know it is: an unproved proposition that imperfectly fulfills the promise of our past but continues to challenge the future.

Democracy, which was a dirty word to our founding fathers, is a precarious and still experimental form of government. There are a lot of things wrong with our version of democracy, in spite of the defensive and near-hysterical adulation to which it moves our professional patriots. The best thing you can say for it is that it works, after a fashion—although in some things it doesn't work as well or as responsively as the British version. And the highest praise the British have found for their form of government is to say that it's probably the best of a number of bad bargains.

I believe in a future in which the United States will become neither a tyranny nor an oligarchy nor a demagoguery, but a true democracy. Before that can happen, its citizens will have to be both free and civilized. They aren't there yet, by a long shot.

I believe in a future in which the United States will take its place among the great and wise powers of the earth, not as the military leader of half the world against the other half but as a giant that can be trusted.

▀▀▀

"How do you feel about being an American, M.?"

"That's your kind of worry, not mine."

"Why not?"

"I'm an internationalist type, old boy; you'll have to ask me how I feel about being a member of the human race."

"How do you feel on that one?"

"Worried. Scared about the whole lot. Scared for some and scared of some. Trying to hope it's all better than it seems. Also that it will last."

"Americans are part of the human race."

"Yup."

▀▀▀

I feel like an American, and a lot of what I feel disgusts me. For instance: the patriotic phoniness of a political rally (very like the equally patriotic phoniness of a football rally).

Toward the end of the 1960 campaign I went to

a political evening in Newark, where an old friend was to make the principal speech. The rendezvous was a judge's house somewhere in one of the Oranges: a medium-sized stucco house crowded with New Jersey politicians, many of the men in evening dress with frilly shirts, their wives gussied up to the nines. I was punctiliously introduced to dozens of people, none of whose names I caught, all of whom got my name immediately. (*That* American trait I admire, in politicians or anybody.) After a buffet supper the party moved on to the rally, in Newark. It was the first time I had ridden in a car with a police escort—screaming sirens, weaving in and out of traffic, through red lights; it was like being royalty or a Red commissar.

The crowd around the barnlike arena in Newark seemed impenetrable; it looked impossible to get out of the car, let alone inside the building. One of my friend's aides said with a pleased smirk that ten thousand of them wouldn't be able to get in. But with police to clear our way, we did. Inside, the air was foul and gray-blue with smoke. Rickety wooden platform, rickety wooden chairs, rickety wooden floor; everybody smoking. If the place caught fire it would be a death trap. And the crowds outside beating on the doors to get in.

The platform filled up with the New Jersey politicians. A band struck up; we all sang "The Star-Spangled Banner," the last two lines with tremendous volume. That was the one good moment of the evening. Then the chairman introduced the speakers and the local politicos. Their faces: cheesy, criminal, sporting, corrupt, greedy, cruel; a rogues' gallery if I ever saw one.

No one could bring the audience to order or silence. They had come to cheer or boo, it hardly mattered which, and whenever a speaker wasn't fawning on their applause or encouraging their jeers they paid no attention; all during the speeches the hall was murmurous with talk and jovial greetings, and the crowd outside kept banging steadily on the doors. Against this drumfire my friend's speech seemed too long, too serious, completely out of key with the rowdy spirit of the audience. Whenever he said "We'll win" or mentioned John F. Kennedy or Nixon he was interrupted and drowned out by enthusiastic mob noises. That was the only kind of thing his listeners wanted to hear or perhaps could take in. As soon as he'd finished, the chairman announced the arrival of FRANK SINATRA—and pandemonium took over. Two screaming women nearly knocked me over getting my chair to stand on and scream some more.

From the platform the aide signaled to me, and I fought my way out of the hall. Police hauled us through the crowds, stuffed us into our official car. The windows were closed and the car's interior was dark; my friend insisted on having the lights on so that he could be seen and recognized, and the window down so that he could shake some of the thrusting hands.

As we drove off behind our police escort through

the tortuous miles of Newark's ghastly night-hung streets, he seemed depressed, and said several times, "Most disagreeable evening." From the front seat his aide kept up a running comment on the plans and commitments for the next two weeks, all of which he had in his head. I said nothing, thinking, with horror, about Hamilton's great beast, the people.

When we got to my friend's hotel he asked me in for a nightcap. I tried to get him to talk about the evening. He said again that it had been "most disagreeable." I said "dreadful" seemed to me a more accurate word. That crowd tonight, multiplied by 100,000—how could anyone believe that its voice could be the voice of common sense or decency? I asked him whether he believed it; he joked it off. But you have to believe it, I said; otherwise how can you believe in the workableness of democracy, how can you believe in what you're doing? He mentioned Jefferson. The people. I said Jefferson's "people" wasn't as bad as that. He seemed to agree. What *can* he believe?

...

We think of ourselves as a nation that produces great men; but our definition of greatness is so debased that we ourselves take it with a grain of salt, half recognizing its cheapness, silliness or inaccuracy. Our Roosevelts, Eisenhowers and Kennedys are never as "great"—or even as good—as we try to believe, nor our Longs, Coughlins and McCarthys as bad as we fear. But we have brought forth a Lincoln; we are also capable of Eichmanns. We had to shoot Lincoln before we acknowledged his worth, and now we have made him into a superhuman myth in order to reassure ourselves that we shall not see his like again. We don't really want another Lincoln; he wouldn't fit into the American setup. Eichmann is more understandable and less foreign to us. For what was Eichmann but an organization man, a loyally functioning ratchet in a great machine?

Evil men, in anything like the absolute sense, have perhaps been rarer in America than in more civilized countries; but the gang and the mob, constantly latent in our loose democracy, are prone to hysterical fear and murderous rage, and always ready for the evil deed. In that aspect, "the people" are indeed a great beast. The political machine, the business corporation, are more neatly organized and more respectably turned out, but they too are amoral, heartless and mindlessly selfish, existing only to secure and further their own existence, and there are no bounds to their greed for power except those enforced on them by law.

Our government itself, were it not fettered by painfully forged safeguards and challenged by the vigilance of individual citizens, would rapidly revert to the tyranny which is its natural state, the government under which most human beings live. A tyranny manufactures, advertises and sells security and order, which everyone wants, at a price which anyone can pay by parting with his "unalienable rights" (how comic that phrase must seem to the dictators!) to his own life, liberty and pursuit of happiness. Where everyone buys, the price does not seem too high—until you have had to pay it.

▄▄▄

Is the United States a religious country? Many Americans will tell you that it is. And they can point to enormous and rising church memberships, rich and powerful churches, etc., etc. You couldn't say of the Americans, as T. S. Eliot has said of the British, that they are "a decent, godless people." In the first place, decency is not the great American virtue, and Americans would hate to be considered godless. (The British don't care.) In this regard, it seems to me that the British have the advantage of us. They admit their own hypocrisy— they are even a little smug about it—when it comes to religion and morals; and they confess that their decency covers a multitude of sins.

In spite of the spectacular gains made by the Roman Catholic Church in the United States, America is still preponderantly a Protestant country. The solemn high point in a Protestant service, corresponding to the elevation of the Host in the Catholic Mass, comes when the offering has been collected and the minister raises the money-filled plate before the altar, while the congregation, rising to its feet, chants the heartfelt Doxology: "Praise God from whom all blessings flow!"

Americans don't like to be considered hypocrites, and would deny the charge until they are blue in the face. So they go on trying to believe that America is, in an almost literal sense, "God's country," and whoop up their anxious faith by evangelistic speeches, and reap their reward in ulcers and coronary thrombosis and nervous breakdowns.

The fact is that Americans do believe in God and in the consolations of religion; but the American god is "free enterprise" and their religion is psychoanalysis.

▴▴▴

Only a generation ago it would have been relatively true to say that American ignorance of the outside world was pretty nearly invincible. In those days, thirty years back, it could be said with some truth that when Americans went abroad they traveled to Cimmeria or Elysium, and always among shades. It was not only Senators and Congressmen who thought of Europe as a lotus land and of Asia as a lowering nightmare. The English, who recognized inferiors everywhere, admitted the real existence of niggers, dagoes, frogs and wogs, when they could be seen, smelled, fended off, ignored or shouted at; but Americans did not really believe in foreigners, even when the foreigners were there. England, as they could see at a glance, was a toy country inhabited by familiar caricatures; Paris was a Freudian dream city where all good American taboos were dead; and so on. It was a child's attitude, but the American idea of the world outside him was a child's idea.

In those days we still attached little value to experience, and we were still almost immune to what we did not understand. We traveled a great deal, but it was always a trip to nowhere. The behavior of Americans in this incredible "abroad" was about what you would expect of children suddenly let loose in a never-never land. Most of them were quickly bored, and wanted to get back to their toys at home; some of them were badly behaved; none of them really believed what they saw, though the politer ones acted as though they did.

The trouble with the world outside America was that it contained a great deal more real life than the guidebooks gave you to understand. It really existed, it had a daily, weekly, continuous being. And the trouble with Americans in such places, especially an American colony or tourist run, was that their collective disbelief in their surroundings gradually leaked out and made them into a social menace: the place sprang into resentful actuality and their dreamy image of it went up in smoke. If they had been content to go there and behave like nice children, pretending that it was a real place, although of course they knew better, all might have been well between it and them. But when the baby pulls the cat's tail once too often he gets scratched. That changes his idea of the cat. And it makes him —ah, how piously we hope it—a more wide-awake baby.

Such thoughts, I admit, were perhaps more applicable to Americans a generation ago, but they still have a certain validity. To some extent we have adopted the old established British attitude: the world of foreigners exists, right enough, but it is an inferior sort of place, and not to be taken too seriously.

16

What'll We Do with the Drunken Sailor?

The drunken sailor in the old chantey is given short shrift: the mildest penalty suggested for him is to "put him in the long boat till he's sober." Is the dissenting American in the same case? If the ship of state is more than a figure of speech, and if all citizens are in fact members of the crew (no passengers allowed on this voyage) then obviously no sea lawyers, scrimshankers or stowaways will be tolerated; every man jack must work his passage and obey orders.

But the metaphor is not yet fact: our democracy has not, so far, turned into a police state. It might happen. If it does, we won't call it a police state but a "new democracy" ("people's democracy" has already been patented by the Communists). It will hardly matter what we call it. Meantime, we suffer dissenters, though not gladly.

The rest of the world fears and resents Americanization as much as we Americans dread conquest by Communism. Home-keeping Americans reject this fact, even as a suggestion. Nevertheless it is a fact.

▾▾▾

What *is* a good American? First of all, he must live in the United States—unless he is serving his country or his company abroad, in enforced exile, and in that case he will count the homesick days until he can return to his native land. If he has not yet reached the age of retirement, he must work at a respectable job, whether he needs the money or not. A good American may retire at the statutory age of sixty-five, although it is more admirable if he doesn't; he may then spend his annuity in Florida, California, Arizona or Hawaii, but he must not settle in foreign parts. A good American must practice togetherness: he must be a family man, a pillar of his community, a loyal member of the team (his company, church, fraternity, college class, etc.). If he is upper-class (i.e., in the higher income brackets) a divorce and a second marriage and a psychoanalysis will not be held against him; on the contrary.

▾▾▾

That ominous farewell they give you in the South: "Come on back, y'heah?" Is it as threatening as it sounds, or is it my wincing imagination? Are they really laying you under some sort of obligation, or reminding you of one? Anyway, that's what it sounds like to me: you've *got* to come back; you'll come back if you know what's good for you. I think all Americans who have wandered from their birthplace—and that includes most of my generation—carry with them a guilty feeling often disguised as "nostalgia." They wouldn't dream of returning to *live* in the house where they were born (even if it hasn't been torn down) but they sometimes feel that "life would have been simpler" if they had. In deeply troubled moments they go even further and wonder whether it might not have been better to stay under the same rooftree their grandfather had. But this is an un-American and almost blasphemous notion, and vanishes like the lightning flash it is.

Progress, betterment, ambition, impatience, restlessness—these have made us wanderers on the face of America. For the fifteen generations of our history, that continental space has given us all the room we wanted; now we are beginning to feel crowded, though we needn't be if we didn't feel impelled to go where the crowds go. When the flood of new settlers has saturated Florida and California and the Southwest, will it leave drained-off regions like the old ghost towns of the West? In some parts of the country the population is static or even shrinking, but just wait: these too will have their turn at being "developed" or redeveloped. Meantime, anyone who chooses to live in one of these high-and-dry places is almost as much out of the swim of present-day America as if he had gone abroad or elected to stay in the past.

▄▄▄

Yes, Americans feel insecure. They have a profound fear of dissolution—death and defeat—which they try to cover by a desperate faith in salvation through "success": free enterprise, good works, the transubstantiation of power into virtue. They have not yet learned like the Europeans to accept the human condition, so their outlook on life seems comparatively childish. But do such comparisons amount to much? In view of the rapidly unfolding terror of the situation in which the whole world finds itself, does it really matter whether we announce over the loudspeaker that all men are brothers or whisper to ourselves that we are like flies which the gods kill for their sport? Since we must come to dust, even the golden lads and lasses, how can that dust be either proud or angry?

We know in part, and we understand in part. How else can we possibly know or understand? No matter who we are, we have only a partial and limited comprehension of what it is to be alive. If we were born American, we have a partial and limited comprehension of what it is to be an American. And yet when we say or think, "I am alive"

or "I am an American," we make the enormous
assumption that for all "practical purposes" we are
as other men are.

The more conscious we may be of the limitations of our experience, the singularity of our nature, the less certainly can we make any general
statement about the limitations and the singularity
of others. Nevertheless, we constantly make such
general statements, for we should be tongue-tied if
we didn't; we somehow scramble over the dilemma
by main force and awkwardness. Though we feel,
with Walt Whitman, that we "contain multitudes,"
that each of us is an unresolved chaos, we act and
talk—and even try to think—as if the conventional
clichés of behavior and speech, the pidgin English
of our daily round, were a satisfactory paraphrase
of the din and discord within us.

...

"Accentuate the positive, eliminate the negative."
That's good American doctrine and lingo both.
Boost, don't knock. Or at any rate be *constructive*.
Instead of standing on the sidelines and making
snide cracks, how about giving us your suggestions? What do you think America should do? Perhaps you've got a program?

O.K., a program. How's this for a starter?

1. Unlimited immigration—refugees preferred.

2. Hand over the Panama Canal to the

United Nations; ditto all military bases in foreign territory.

3. Turn our colonies loose (Puerto Rico, the Virgin Islands and any others I've forgotten) whenever they want their independence.

4. Amend the Constitution to make it a felony for any man to offer himself for President.

5. Change the election rules: President and Congress to be elected together every five years.

6. Declare war on Mexico and make the Mexicans take Texas back.

7. Concentrate the educational system on teaching all Americans to read and write before they are fifteen (those glamour girls, mathematics and science, will take care of themselves).

▀▀▀

What am I trying to say? That after sixty years of a lucky and protected life I know how to live, or how to be an American? That after a three-month trip through a small part of the United States I can tell my fellow Americans what's wrong with the country? No, none of those things.

A younger friend of mine said to me after reading part of this manuscript, "Who's *interested* in a bookful of your annoyances on a trumped-up trip? If you're going to criticize a country, you'd better live in it. You want a title? *Running Down America.*"

I'll tell you what the tone is: it's disapproval. An air of disapproval is not like outdoor air and sunshine, or fresh rain falling. Nothing like at all. If you can't be outdoor air, and you won't be sunshine, couldn't you at least be fresh rain falling?"

The answer, the regretful answer, must be, "No, I guess not." Much as I might like to be a breath of outdoor air or a wink of sunshine, or a brief shower of fresh rain falling, those wishful metaphors do not apply to me. But in spite of my unfilial and disapproving remarks, America is my father and mother. Like the lady who decided to accept the universe, I accept the United States; and, by God, sir, I'd better. What else is there for me to accept? I'm not going to shoot myself or become a citizen of another country or try to overthrow the government. The fact is, I am simply exercising the right of every American to be an annoyance, within legal limits.

Nobody has to pay attention; nobody has to read me. And I'm under no illusions about the small number of people who will, or about the weight or extent of any influence I might have on them. There will never be enough of me to make a dent on any political party or swing an election—well, maybe a very small election, perhaps a school board. I don't like organizations of any kind; the anarchists have always seemed to me to have the right idea. And I suspect there are a good many other Americans like me, though not enough to matter. We think capital and labor, church, state and community are rotten with organization. Another friend of mine believes, or tries to believe, that individual Americans, the old-style "rugged individualists," still exist in such numbers that they form the backbone if not the dominant minority of the country. I think he's whistling in the dark.

The official line, apparently accepted by the vast majority of Americans, is that our present peril lies in the inescapable fact that we are on a collision course with Russia. But the true state of affairs (which is always different from the official line) is worse than that: America is on a collision course with itself. The United States is in process of becoming conformist, reactionary, the beleaguered champion of the *status quo ante*—the very opposite of the kind of nation it set out to be.

▴▴▴

Then what have I tried to say? "My country, right or wrong, but right or wrong my country"? That's about it—with qualifications. The main qualification is that the most audible sounds and the most prominently visible sights in America today are about as wrong, in my view and to my ears, as they could be. I believe that the American idea is still on trial—as much on trial as it was when Lincoln spoke at Gettysburg. I do not think our nation can long endure unless the dwindling minority of ornery Americans stops dwindling and becomes again a force of opinion to be reckoned with.

Our nation was dedicated to a noble experiment.

Its founders wanted the United States to be the best country on earth: not necessarily the richest or strongest, but the best for civilized human beings to live in. I hope and try to believe, against an increasing weight of evidence, that our American experiment might yet succeed.

ABOUT THE AUTHOR

Born in Ohio at the turn of the century, T. S. Matthews was educated at a military academy, at St. Paul's School, at Princeton, and at Oxford. His career as a journalist—first with the New Republic *and later as editor of* Time *Magazine—was punctuated by the publication of several novels as well as poetry. His most recent books have been* The Sugar Pill, *a critique of journalism as it is practiced today, and his autobiography,* Name and Address.